CAMBRIDGE LIBRARY COLLECTION

Books of enduring scholarly value

Polar Exploration

This series includes accounts, by eye-witnesses and contemporaries, of early expeditions to the Arctic and the Antarctic. Huge resources were invested in such endeavours, particularly the search for the North-West Passage, which, if successful, promised enormous strategic and commercial rewards. Cartographers and scientists travelled with many of the expeditions, and their work made important contributions to earth sciences, climatology, botany and zoology. They also brought back anthropological information about the indigenous peoples of the Arctic region and the southern fringes of the American continent. The series further includes dramatic and poignant accounts of the harsh realities of working in extreme conditions and utter isolation in bygone centuries.

Rear Admiral Sir John Franklin

Sir John Ross (1777–1856), the distinguished British naval officer and Arctic explorer, undertook three great voyages to the Arctic regions; accounts of his first and his second voyages are also reissued in this series. (During the latter, his ship was stranded in the unexplored area of Prince Regent Inlet, where Ross and his crew survived by living and eating as the local Inuit did.) In this volume, first published in 1855, the explorer describes his experiences during his third (privately funded) Arctic voyage, undertaken in 1850 as part of the effort to locate the missing expedition led by Sir John Franklin, his close friend. Ross also summarises in partisan style the previous efforts by the Royal Navy to find out what happened to the *Erebus* and *Terror*, and is scathing in his account of what he regards as the mismanagement and incompetence of the Admiralty.

Cambridge University Press has long been a pioneer in the reissuing of out-of-print titles from its own backlist, producing digital reprints of books that are still sought after by scholars and students but could not be reprinted economically using traditional technology. The Cambridge Library Collection extends this activity to a wider range of books which are still of importance to researchers and professionals, either for the source material they contain, or as landmarks in the history of their academic discipline.

Drawing from the world-renowned collections in the Cambridge University Library and other partner libraries, and guided by the advice of experts in each subject area, Cambridge University Press is using state-of-the-art scanning machines in its own Printing House to capture the content of each book selected for inclusion. The files are processed to give a consistently clear, crisp image, and the books finished to the high quality standard for which the Press is recognised around the world. The latest print-on-demand technology ensures that the books will remain available indefinitely, and that orders for single or multiple copies can quickly be supplied.

The Cambridge Library Collection brings back to life books of enduring scholarly value (including out-of-copyright works originally issued by other publishers) across a wide range of disciplines in the humanities and social sciences and in science and technology.

Rear Admiral
Sir John Franklin

A Narrative of the Circumstances and Causes
Which Led to the Failure of the Searching
Expeditions Sent By Government and Others
for the Rescue of Sir John Franklin

JOHN ROSS

CAMBRIDGE
UNIVERSITY PRESS

CAMBRIDGE UNIVERSITY PRESS

Cambridge, New York, Melbourne, Madrid, Cape Town,
Singapore, São Paolo, Delhi, Mexico City

Published in the United States of America by Cambridge University Press, New York

www.cambridge.org
Information on this title: www.cambridge.org/9781108049788

© in this compilation Cambridge University Press 2012

This edition first published 1855
This digitally printed version 2012

ISBN 978-1-108-04978-8 Paperback

REAR ADMIRAL

SIR JOHN FRANKLIN,

C.B.　　　　　　　　K.C.H.

A NARRATIVE,

ETC.

BY

REAR-ADMIRAL SIR JOHN ROSS, C.B., K.C.S., K.S.A., &c.

"MAGNA EST VERITAS, ET PRÆVALEBIT."

LONDON:

LONGMANS, GREEN, BROWN, & LONGMANS,

PATERNOSTER ROW.

1855.

SHIPS SEEN ON THE 20TH APRIL, 1851, SUPPOSED TO BE THE EREBUS AND TERROR.

REAR ADMIRAL

SIR JOHN FRANKLIN,

C.B.   K.C.H.

A NARRATIVE

OF

THE CIRCUMSTANCES AND CAUSES WHICH LED TO THE FAILURE
OF THE SEARCHING EXPEDITIONS SENT BY GOVERNMENT
AND OTHERS FOR THE RESCUE OF SIR
JOHN FRANKLIN.

BY

REAR-ADMIRAL SIR JOHN ROSS, C.B., K.C.S., K.S.A., &c.

"MAGNA EST VERITAS, ET PRÆVALEDIT."

LONDON:
LONGMANS, GREEN, BROWN, & LONGMANS,
PATERNOSTER ROW.
1855.

LONDON :
H. SILVERLOCK, PRINTER, WARDROBE TERRACE,
DOCTORS' COMMONS.

TO

𝕿𝖍𝖊 𝕲𝖔𝖛𝖊𝖗𝖓𝖔𝖗 𝖆𝖓𝖉 𝕯𝖎𝖗𝖊𝖈𝖙𝖔𝖗𝖘

OF

THE HONOURABLE THE HUDSON BAY COMPANY,

BY WHOSE SYMPATHY AND MUNIFICENCE THE AUTHOR
WAS ENABLED TO REDEEM HIS PLEDGE,

BY EQUIPPING AN EXPEDITION IN SEARCH OF SIR JOHN FRANKLIN
AND HIS DEVOTED COMPANIONS,

THIS NARRATIVE

IS, BY PERMISSION,

𝕯𝖊𝖉𝖎𝖈𝖆𝖙𝖊𝖉,

BY THEIR OBLIGED AND GRATEFUL SERVANT,

JOHN ROSS, *Rear-Admiral.*

INTRODUCTION.

THE name of Sir John Franklin is so well known and appreciated, that any comment of mine on the career of that distinguished officer must be unnecessary. In justice, however, to those who may not be acquainted with the formation of our friendship and intimacy, as well as my reasons for taking so deep an interest in his rescue, I feel called upon to inform my readers, that our first acquaintance commenced in the year 1818, when he was appointed lieutenant commanding the *Trent* discovery vessel, then fitting out under my directions, and subsequently under the orders of Captain Buchan in the *Dorothea*, in their attempt to reach the North Pole, which ended in serious damage to both vessels, and during the two memorable journeys which he performed with that unflinching perseverance for which he has always been distinguished. Our intimacy continued during other services on which he was employed, but the deep interest he took in my rescue, from a hitherto unparalleled voyage of difficulty and danger, finally and completely cemented our mutual friendship and esteem, and it was with sorrow I witnessed his embarkation on a service rendered peculiarly desperate from the disadvantages hereafter mentioned, and in return for his humane and noble conduct I gladly availed myself of the opportunity of assuring him that, although advanced in years, I would without fail volunteer for his rescue, which I was too sure would be eventually necessary. With this view, and having to return to Stockholm, in 1846, to settle my affairs in that city, I proposed an expedition for measuring an arc of the meridian at

Spitzbergen, on which service I had secured the assistance of the talented son of the celebrated Professor Schumacher, intimating at the same time that my expedition could return, in the summer of 1847, in time for a search for the missing ships. Urging that the season was extremely favourable, my plans were referred to the Hydrographer, but there was a malevolent influence at the Admiralty, which could not be overcome, and the puerile and absurd excuse, " no time to prepare instruments," was made the poor reason of a negative. The gallant Franklin sailed on the 23rd of May, 1845, was last heard of July in the same year, and for reference to the reader, I give a list of the officers and crews, of both the *Erebus* and *Terror*, with the Admiralty Instructions; and I have only to add, that my object is to disabuse the public touching the causes of failure, and every circumstance relating to the endeavours which have been made for the rescue of the brave officers and men whose melancholy fate has excited the sympathy not only of the United Kingdom, but of Europe and America, while I trust it will be seen that I have, with as little offence as possible, redeemed the sacred pledge I gave to my ever-to-be-lamented friend and brother officer.

JOHN ROSS,

Rear-Admiral.

THE FRANKLIN EXPEDITION.

THE period having now arrived when the public must expect from me an exposition of every circumstance relative to the rescue of Sir John Franklin and his companions, as far as I have been concerned in such unfortunate and unsuccessful operations, the more especially as it is known that I pledged myself, by a sacred promise to Sir John Franklin, that I would do all in my power for their rescue, it is not without reluctance, as well as concern, that I find myself in a position where my opinions may be found so widely at variance with those of several of my brother officers as to be anything but complimentary to their decisions, while they must also appear no less uncongenial to those feelings of others on whom the responsibility of the vital proceedings rests.

But this is an occasion on which not only the truth, but the whole truth, is imperatively demanded, and on which I shall enter without fear of contradiction, and equally regardless of the consequences. My object is, without giving offence, to prove that, in the first place, I have duly performed the sacred promise which I made to my gallant friend, in return for the deep interest he took for my rescue under similar circumstances; and, secondly, that my opinions and plans were right and ought to have been adopted; and, lastly, that my experience and know ledge ought not to have been treated with that consummate disregard, which must appear manifest throughout this narrative; but in this free and enlightened country the truth will always be triumphant.

I shall begin with the cause and history of the Franklin Expedition for the Discovery of the North-West Passage. Ten years had passed since my return from an expedition designated by the Admiralty as unparalleled, &c.; and the interest excited on that occasion had, as in all such cases, died away. Meanwhile, pains were taken by certain individuals belonging to the Royal Society, to throw some doubt on part of my narrative, while others were jealous of the honours that had been bestowed on me. The nation was at peace with all the world, and on the 12th December, 1844, another attempt for the discovery of the north-west passage was proposed by the Council of the Royal Society, and sanctioned in due time by the Admiralty. It was reported that my nephew, Sir James Clark Ross, was to have the command, but if that was the case, he declined it, when a volunteer was soon found in the gallant Franklin, then fifty-eight years of age, and two ships, the *Erebus* and *Terror*, that had returned from the Antarctic expedition, were selected, and were nearly ready for sea when I returned from Stockholm, in February, 1845. I have now to show that Franklin laboured under great disadvantages; in the first place, his ships were too large, the addition of steam-machinery, in such a class of vessel, took up much of her stowage, and brought the ships deeper in their draught of water; but worst of all, they were supplied with Goldner's canisters of meat, which were (as subsequently proved to be) putrid and unfit for human food.

It was not long before I had communication with my old and valued friend, when I informed him that the winter of 1844-5 had been very severe, that I came from Helsingborg to Elsinore in a carriage with four horses, that when I passed Hamburg they were roasting an ox on the Elbe, and that I had to come by Rotterdam to get to England, and that consequently he could not expect to get farther this season than Cornwallis Island. At a subsequent meeting he told me, that other officers were of opinion that, although the winter was severe in Sweden and Denmark, it might not be so in Baffin's Bay, but it was in vain I told him, that I had examined the records of St. Petersburg, Stockholm, Copenhagen, and Archangel for forty years, and it was invariably found that whenever it was severe in these places, the winter was also severe in Baffin's Bay; but other officers were of a different opinion, and that was by him deemed satisfactory! I may here observe, that neither the Government nor those consulted ever took into consideration the mildness or the severity of the preceding winters, which is absolutely necessary in order to judge of the navigation and state of the sea and ice during the succeeding summer.

On several occasions, I had conversations with Sir John Franklin about being frozen in, and related to him that by leaving a *dépôt* of provisions, as we proceeded on our voyage in the *Victory*, we had saved our lives, and I enjoined him to adopt the same plan, and if possible to leave a boat or two. He replied, he could not spare boats. Two days before the *Erebus* left Woolwich I had a long conversation with him, when he told me his orders; and when, after repeating to him that he would be surely frozen in near Cornwallis Island, I said, " Has any one volunteered to follow you ?" He replied, " No, none." " Has not my nephew volunteered ?" " No, he has promised his wife's relations that he will not go to sea any more—Back is unwell—and Parry has a good appointment." " Then," I said, " I shall volunteer to look for you, if you are not heard of in February, 1847 ; but pray put a notice in the cairn where you winter, *if you do proceed*, which of the routes you take."

After this conversation, I met him at his lodgings in London, and reiterated the same request; and, lastly, when I took final leave of him, we shook hands, and his last words were—" Ross, you are the only one who has volunteered to look for me; God bless you." I need scarcely add, that I repeated and expressed my most sacred promise that I should not fail to perform, and it now remains to be seen whether I have done my utmost to redeem my pledge!

During the remainder of the year 1845, my attention was occupied in the settlement of my private affairs, but it did not preclude me from observing the progress and state of the approaching winter, which in this country was certainly much milder than the preceding one. I therefore judged that the expedition would winter in Barrow's Strait, or, possibly, at Melville Island, and taking advantage of open water, consequent on the mild season, would push on in the execution of his orders, and being fully convinced that all would depend on his success during that season, the summer and autumn of 1846, it was with the utmost anxiety I saw myself obliged to wait for the month of January, 1847, before which no tidings could be reasonably expected. In the summer of 1846, I went to North-West Castle, my residence in Scotland, where I had private affairs to settle, which detained me until autumn, when I returned to London.

The ships *Erebus* and *Terror*, the former of 378 tons, and the latter (formerly a bomb-vessel) of 326 tons, were the same as were employed under Captain Sir J. C. Ross, in the Antarctic Expedition; and the latter, also the same as commanded by Captain Back in the ice at Hudson's Bay, proved on both occasions to be totally unfit for such a service, were now commanded, officered, and manned, and sailed (at the instance of Sir J. Barrow), as follows:—

EREBUS.

Sir John Franklin, *Captain.*
James Fitzjames, *Commander.*
Graham Gore, ⎫
H. T. D. Le Visconte, ⎬ *Lieutenants.*
J. W. Fairholme, ⎭
Ch. F. de Væux, ⎫
Robert O. Sargent, ⎬ *Mates.*
Edward Couch, ⎭
H. F. Collins, *Second Master.*
Stephen Stanley, *Surgeon.*
H. B. Goodsir, *Assistant Surgeon.*
C. H. Osmer, *Paymaster.*
James Reid, *Ice Master.*
12 Warrant and Petty Officers.
53 Seamen and Marines.
———
70 Total.

TERROR.

Richard Crozier, *Captain.*
Edward Little, ⎫
G. H. Hodgson, ⎬ *Lieutenants.*
John Irving, ⎭
Frederick Hornby, ⎫
Robert Thomas, ⎬ *Mates.*
Thomas Blanky, *Ice Master.*
MacBean *Second Master.*
John Peddie, *Surgeon.*

Alexander M'Donald, *Assistant Surgeon*.
J. Helpman, *Clerk in Charge*.
11 Warrant and Petty Officers.
57 Seamen and Marines.
___

68 Total.

Grand Total, 138.

[For Sir John Franklin's official instructions, see Appendix, A.]

In the autumn of the year 1846, Captains in the Royal
Navy were peremptorily called upon to decide on taking
the retirement, and being senior to the prescribed time
(1825), I was of course entitled to it, and might have
retired with the offered guinea per day, but my sacred
promise to Franklin prevented me, as it would have
incapacitated me from taking the command of any
Government expedition. The answer to my first letter
having been evasive, I therefore wrote a second to the
Admiralty, declining to accept the retirement in consequence of my promise to volunteer to search for him
if not heard of in February, 1847, for which I had a
flattering acknowledgment; and having no doubt that my
services would be accepted, I remained without making
any further application until the time should arrive, while
the retirement took place on the 1st of October, 1846,
when I found my name within sixty of the top of the list
of captains, and very few senior to me actually employed.
The return home of Sir John Franklin was now anxiously
expected, but at the end of the month, when all hope of
that was at an end, the cry was, Oh! he has got through,
and we shall hear of him through the Sandwich Islands,
viâ Mazatalan, in January; and my having expressed some
doubts of his success, brought down upon me the censure
and opprobrium of all the opposite party, and through
them the indignation of Sir John Franklin's *best friend*.
Besides my pamphlet in refutation of Sir John Barrow's
misrepresentations, which caused the tide to turn in my
favour, the return of Dr. John Rae, who had been
quietly employed to explore the space to the S. E. of the
Isthmus of Boothia, of which expedition neither Sir J.
Barrow nor Sir J. C. Ross had any knowledge, confirming
all that I had asserted, and which by these gentlemen
had been unwarrantably denied, turned the tide so com-

pletely in my favour, that anything appeared to them better than to allow me to command any expedition for the rescue of Franklin, and steps were taken accordingly. Anxious, however, to obtain all the information possible, and being also obliged to give up my appointment as Consul at Stockholm, which I had resigned, and to settle my affairs there, I took Lady Ross to Balkail, where I left her, during my absence with my brother-in-law, Mr. Adair, and proceeded *viâ* Edinburgh first in a small vessel to Norway, then to Gothenburg, and eventually to Stockholm, where I remained during the month of June.

Before leaving London, however, on the 28th May, 1846, I conceived a plan of combining the relief of Franklin with the measurement of an arc of the meridian at Spitzbergen, on which subject I had a communication with my friend, Professor Schumacher.

Having arrived safely in London with my little yacht the *Mary*, assisted by only one seaman, I had her hauled up at Woolwich by permission of Admiral Dundas, in Woolwich Dock-yard. Intending her as my retreat vessel should I be so fortunate as to obtain the command of an expedition for the rescue of the missing ships, I wrote the following letter to the Secretary, which I have before alluded to, on the subject of retirement.

16, Park-street, Grosvenor-square, Sept. 28, 1846.

SIR,

Having promised to Sir John Franklin that, in the event of the Expedition under his command being frozen in (as the one I directed was for four years), I would volunteer in 1847 to proceed to certain positions we had agreed upon in search of him and his brave companions, I request you will be pleased to inform me if their Lordships would consider my accepting the retirement a bar to my being appointed to any ship or vessel that may be ordered on that service.

I have, &c.,
JOHN ROSS.

W. A. B. Hamilton, Captain, R.N., Secretary, &c. &c.

To this I received the following answer from the Secretary of the Admiralty.

Admiralty, Sept. 30, 1846.

Sir,

I have received and laid before my Lords Commissioners of the Admiralty your letter of the 28th instant, and I am to acquaint you in reply, that although your gallant and humane intentions are fully appreciated by their Lordships, yet no such service is at present contemplated by my Lords, and they have not, therefore, taken into consideration the appointment of an officer to conduct it.

I have, &c.

(Signed)   W. A. B. HAMILTON.

Sir John Ross, C.B., 16, Park-street, Grosvenor-square.

This reply, like others I received from the same quarter, was evasive, and doubtless in order to induce me to accept the retirement and thereby throw me on the shelf. But I lost no time in writing to refuse the proffered retirement, although it would have raised my pay from 14s. 6d. to 20s. per day, and given me in a year or more the *rank* of Rear-Admiral. My letter, which was duly acknowledged, need not be inserted; the question, therefore, was finally settled, and this therefore could not be a bar to my employment on that or any other service.

Having returned from Stockholm, after settling my affairs there, and delivering my consulate to my successor, Major Pringle, I still held to the purpose of my expedition. I put into Calmar for refreshment and for some alterations to enable me to cross the North Sea; I reached Elsinore, and from thence sailed to England in fourteen days. On my arrival in England I wrote a letter to Rear-Admiral Beaufort, from which the following is an extract:—

"The whole of the Arctic Seas have been free from ice in less than six weeks sooner than ever known or recorded, and from the experience I have had during my long residence in Sweden, in travelling by sledges, I have no doubt of complete success, and requesting that my proposal may be communicated to their Lordships."

P.S. Since writing the above, I have communicated with Doctor (formerly Captain) Scoresby, who was the first to propose the principle, and he has authorized me to say that he highly approves of my modification, which he considers so great an improvement as to secure complete success, while the expedition would return next year in good time to proceed in search of the expedition under Sir John Franklin, if found to be necessary.

JOHN ROSS.

In answer to this letter, I received the following letter from Sir F. Beaufort, Hydrographer to the Admiralty :

Admiralty, May 21, 1846.

DEAR SIR JOHN,

I have attentively read your letter of this morning, and I have had some conversation with Sir George Cockburn on the subject. With your probability of reaching the Pole by means of Swedish sledges I will not meddle ; but I confess the only temptation to me in the whole scheme is the measurement of an arc of the meridian at Spitzbergen, and that would require so many instruments to be prepared, so many arrangements made, before you could start, and so many observers to accompany you, that I could not in conscience urge him to comply with your request.

I am, yours truly,
FRANCIS BEAUFORT.

To Sir John Ross, C.B., &c.

It was cold water in the outset thrown on my whole scheme, but it occurred to me that I might induce Sir Francis to reconsider the subject, and on my arrival at Leith, on my way to sail for Norway and Sweden for the purposes already mentioned, I wrote to him again, but still without success.

It was on the 19th May, after having been several days at Greenhithe in the Thames, to go through the farce of having the ships' compasses adjusted, that the ships sailed, and were towed by the steamers north about until they were fairly in the Atlantic ocean. The expedition, consisting of the *Erebus* and *Terror*, was preceded by the transport *Barretto Junior*, which might at that season of the year have easily carried out a small vessel such as Penny had on the Polar expedition, but my suggestion to that effect was also disregarded. Each of the discovery ships was fitted with screw propellers, the effect of which, besides materially weakening the stern-post and after-frame of the ship, had the disadvantage of taking up a great deal of room necessary for both the machinery and fuel, which ought to have been devoted to a larger supply of provisions. It was in vain that I pointed out that a small steam vessel, such as the *Victory*, would be much more efficient, less expensive, and would enable the ships to carry more provisions, as she might either be sent home or retained as a retreat vessel.

Sir John Franklin was last seen by the whaler, *Prince of Wales*, on the 26th July, 1845, in lat. 74°43′ north, and long. 66°16′ west, a position which fully proved that his progress would not be more than I had anticipated, and much less than the average passages as published by Dr. Scoresby, while it does not appear that any use had been made of his screw propeller; on that day both ships were fast to an iceberg, waiting for an opening in them, and the crews of both ships in high spirits.

During the intervening period between the departure of the expedition on the 23rd of May, 1845, and February, 1847, my attention was particularly given to the state of the weather. I corresponded with my friends in Sweden, Denmark, and Russia, as well as with the masters of ships returning from the fishery in Baffin's Bay, and it was with sorrow I found all unanimous in representing the winter of 1845-6 to be more than usually severe, and, by accounts from the latter, that the "land-ice" extended from the west coast further than they had seen it; and on my return to Stockholm, in 1846, to give up my consulship and settle my affairs, I found their report to be true, and there could be, therefore, little chance of the ships making any progress during the autumn of 1846. My observations on the state of the weather continued, and it was with satisfaction I ascertained that the winter of 1846-7 was mild, that vessels had left Stockholm on the 1st of January, and had passed through the Sound as late as the middle of that month; consequently, that I had a fair prospect of being able to complete the relief or rescue (in the case of accident) of my gallant friend, to whom I had pledged my word, especially as it was now evident that he had not found or accomplished the north-west passage. My plans were therefore prepared with a chart denoting the probable place where the expedition would be found, namely, in the neighbourhood of Cornwallis Island; and when the time arrived, the 9th of February, 1847—never doubting that, as I was the only volunteer, my services would be readily accepted—I repaired to the Admiralty with my documents, which I gave into the hands of Captain Hamilton,* the Secretary, who forthwith took them to the Board then sitting, and in a short time he returned, and re-delivered them to me with the following verbal message:—" Their Lordships have desired me to inform you that they have already consulted and taken the opinions of Sir John Barrow, Sir Edward Parry, Sir James C. Ross, Colonel Sabine, Doctor Richardson, and others, who were unanimously of opinion that it was quite unnecessary to send out an expedition of relief in that year." I cannot doubt but that these individuals had given their opinions conscientiously, believing that if the expedition did not succeed, that it might return ; but as they did not take into their consideration that the ships had already been frozen in during two severe winters, probably in the same spot, that they might not be extricated until very late in the autumn, when the navigation of that sea is in the last degree dangerous, I need scarcely add that I was mortified, not only at the unexpected refusal to my application, but that the Board (at which, I believe, the first Lord was not present) declined even to hear what I had to say. Determined, however, that the opportunity should not be lost, because it was more than probable the next season would be severe, I wrote the following letter to Sir Charles Adam, the first sea Lord, after an interview I had with him at the Admiralty, on the 9th of February, 1847 :

16, Park-street, Grosvenor-square, Feb. 9, 1847.

Sir,

In reference to the communication I had the honour of making to you this morning, when I pointed out the impossibility of Sir John Franklin and his crews being able to reach the nearest place where a whaling ship was to be found, from the position in which the expedition must be frozen up, consequent on the known intention of Sir John Franklin to put his ships into the drift ice at the western end of Cornwallis or Melville Island, a risk which was deemed in a high degree imprudent by Lieut. Parry and the Officers of the Expedition of 1819-20, with ships of a less draught of water, and in every respect better calculated to withstand the pressure of the ice, and other dangers to which they must be exposed ; and as it is now evident that the expedition cannot have succeeded in passing Behring's Strait, and, if not

* See copy of my letter to Captain Hamilton.

totally lost, that the ships must have been carried by the ice that is known to drift to the southward, on land seen at a great distance in that direction, and from which position the accumulation of ice will, as in my own case, for ever prevent the return of the ships; consequently, they must be abandoned either on the 1st of May or soon after, in order to reach Melville or Cornwallis Island about the end of June, and where they must remain until the 1st of August, and at which places I had selected for them to leave a *dépôt* of provisions, absolutely necessary for their sustenance ; or, if they defer their journey until the 1st of May, 1848, it would be still more requisite that provisions and boats should be left by them at that *dépôt*, which it would also be my intention to do, after having secured my ship in a harbour on the west side of Barrow's Strait, in such a position as would enable them to reach a point where the sea (in August) was sufficiently open for boats to leave their position at Winter Harbour or elsewhere ; in the meantime, I would survey the west coast of Boothia, which has not yet been determined ; in addition to the acknowledgment of my letter of the 27th ult., informing me that my letters had been received and laid before the Board, I was officially informed by Captain Hamilton, that in consequence of the opinions of my nephew, Sir James Clark Ross, and others, it was not the intention of their Lordships to accede to my proposal, but to offer a reward to whaling ships and the Hudson's Bay Company, to use their endeavours for the rescue of Franklin and his companions, a proposition I hereby protest against as utterly inefficient, and characterise as disingenuous as it is absurd, and which I believe must have been suggested by unworthy motives, for Sir J. C. Ross is one of those officers who, in Parry's expedition, was *then* of opinion that what Sir John Franklin intended to do was imprudent, and who from experience knew with what extreme difficulty we travelled five hundred miles, over much smoother ice, to gain Fury Beach. He must be certain that Franklin and his men, 138 in number, could not travel 600 miles, while we had the *Fury's* boats and her stores to maintain us in prospect ; but unless we reach their position either at Cornwallis or Melville Island, they will have nothing ! The principal object, however, of this letter is, respectfully to suggest that your Lordships would be pleased to refer my proposition to the President and Council of the Royal Society, who recommended the expedition of Sir John Franklin, and also to the Royal Astronomical and Geographical Societies, which, while it would relieve your Lordships of a heavy responsibility, would be so far satisfactory,—even if their opinions are in opposition to mine, namely, that it is absolutely necessary for the rescue of our gallant countrymen that an expedition for that purpose should be sent from hence in June next,—because it will prove that, as far as lay in my power, I have conscientiously performed my sacred promise.

> I have the honour to be, with the highest respect,
> Your obedient, humble servant,
> JOHN ROSS, Captain, R.N.

To the above letter I received the following brief reply from Sir Charles Adam:

Admiralty, Feb. 11, 1847.

DEAR SIR JOHN,

In reply to your letter of the 9th instant, I have only to inform you that, since the expedition under the command of Sir John Franklin was undertaken at the instance of the Royal Society, that body should make the application to the Admiralty.

> Yours truly,
> CHARLES ADAM.

It may be here noticed that no reply is made to the most important part of my letter, but it will be hereafter shown how it was both noticed and most unwarrantably misrepresented. I had now no alternative but to communicate on the subject with the Marquis of Northampton, then President of the Royal Society, a nobleman well known as a patron of science as also for the urbanity of his manners. But my interview with him was somewhat extraordinary. When I first laid my chart before his Lordship, and proceeded to say that I was a volunteer to perform my promise to search for my friend, his Lordship replied, "You will go and get frozen in like Franklin, and we shall have to send after you!" Astonished at such a remark, I said, "Surely your Lordship cannot mean that no search shall be made for Franklin and his brave companions?" His Lordship, after looking at the chart, then said that the new council would be elected in a few days, and that he would submit my letter* and plan of search to it soon after the election, and that I should be informed of the result. It was, however, too evident that his Lordship was not favourable to my project; and when I found that some of the very persons who have given a negative advice to the Admiralty, composed the council, I had little hope of success, and was not surprised when I received the following disingenuous answer to my appli-

---

* See Appendix, B, 12th February, 1847.

cation. " The President and Council of the Royal Society
do not think it proper to give their opinion on the subject of your letter, unless especially required to do so by
the Admiralty!" Thus was the most valuable and important period which, properly used, by means of prompt
measures, might have led to most important results in the
cause of humanity and science, frittered away and irre-
trievably lost in a puerile and petty squabble between
the Royal Society and the Board of Admiralty! The
Astronomical and Geographical Societies, who in such
instances follow the decisions of the Royal, being in some
degree constituted of the same individual members, were
applied to, but of course without success. But I had
some hope of my plans, with a little variation, being
entertained by the British Association for the Advancement of Science, which was held at Oxford in that year.
Thither I repaired, and being a member, I was also supported by Dr. Lee, LL.D., who took great interest in the
success of my application, which was, however, unfortunately submitted to a section composed principally of
the same individuals who had previously given their veto
against it, although it will be seen as follows that it was
so worded as to meet the true objects of the Association.
But before I took this step I had the following correspondence with the Marquis of Northampton.

The object of this letter being first to protest against
further delay, and then that the subject should be immediately referred to the President and Council of the Royal
Society, that had been the cause of Sir John Franklin's
expedition, I lost no time in procuring a *second* interview
with the Marquis of Northampton, as President of the
Royal Society, and delivered to his Lordship, at his
house in Piccadilly, the following letter :—

16, Park-street, Feb. 15, 1847.
My Lord,

I have the honour to inform your Lordship that I had, during the last spring, for the double purpose of measuring an arc of the meridian at Spitzbergen and making another attempt to reach the North Pole, which was to have been undertaken at the expense of my patriotic friend Sir Felix Booth, but which was subsequently abandoned by him in consequence of the animadversions contained in the late publication of Sir John Barrow, who he thought might impute to him sinister motives. In May last, I addressed a letter to the talented Hydrographer of the Admiralty, at the desire of the Earl of Haddington, the extract of which I enclose, and will fully explain my plan, which, for obvious reasons, was never acted upon.

I have been induced to renew my application to my Lords Commissioners of the Admiralty mainly from the fact of my having promised to Sir John Franklin that I would volunteer to rescue him and his brave companions if not heard of in the spring of 1847, and the probability (nothing having been heard of his expedition by the whalers, now all arrived from Baffin's Bay) is, that the ships are either frozen up or that some misfortune has befallen them.

My proposal is, therefore, that an expedition should be prepared, such as in that extract of my letter to Admiral Beaufort, and that if no accounts are received of Sir John Franklin's expedition before the 1st of July, 1847, the expedition should proceed to Lancaster Sound, in search of that gallant officer and the men employed in ascertaining the existence or otherwise of a north-west passage.

But if, on the contrary, the expedition returns by that time, or if it has happily passed Behring's Straits, then the expedition under my command will proceed to Spitzbergen, in order to perform the service I have described. Having pointed out to their Lordships how the expedition could be fitted out at a very moderate expense, I have earnestly stated the necessity of commencing the fitting out the expedition, first, because it will be absolutely necessary to provide Lapland clothing for those who are to be employed in travelling to search for Sir John Franklin and his companions, and in travelling to the Pole, and this kind of clothing can only be procured during the winter through Consul-General Crowe, at Christiana, in Norway; secondly, the steam machinery for the vessel I have selected, the fitting out of which will require considerable time.

Trusting that your Lordship's candour will excuse my zeal in the advancement of science and geographical knowledge, and do justice to the sincerity of my desire to rescue the gallant officers and men who are now looking forward to the promise I made of rendering them assistance, I venture to request that your Lordship, as President of the Royal Society, will be pleased to submit my proposal to the Council, and by taking it into favourable consideration, transmit to me your high approval and recommendation. I have now only to express my unqualified readiness to receive any communication made to me by your Lordship or the Royal Society, and to pay every attention to their wishes that lies in my power ; and I am, with the highest respect, my Lord, your Lordship's most obedient and humble servant,

John Ross, Captain, Royal Navy.

Right Hon. the Marquis of Northampton, &c. &c. &c.

I waited again on the Marquis of Northampton, according to appointment, and was most graciously received by his Lordship, who attentively perused my letter, but after doing justice to my desire to rescue the officers and men of the missing expedition, he repeated in nearly the same words as used on a former occasion, " It will be of no use sending you by sea to search for Franklin; you will be frozen in as he is, and we should have to send after you, and then perhaps for them that went to look for you!" I replied, "Surely your Lordship does not mean to say that no steps should be taken to rescue Franklin?" His Lordship then said that he would lay my letter before the Council, but as a new Council was to be elected at the next meeting of the Royal Society, he would wait until the new Council had taken their seats. His Lordship then mentioned a land expedition, of the inefficacy of which I soon convinced him.

I then pointed out to his Lordship three different causes of failure of the efforts of Franklin, first, that due consideration had not been given to the state of the previous winter, which in Sweden and America was more than usually severe, having myself travelled from Stockholm to London in the February of that year, when I crossed the Sound, Belt, and the Elbe on the ice, and was finally obliged to take the route through Germany and Holland, and cross viâ Rotterdam and Helvoetsluys. The second disadvantage was the large size of the two ships, which had been proved by the loss of the *Fury* to be a decided fault, as by drawing, like her, more water than the ice, they would be liable to damage from grounding before the mass of ice when beset in it, and if damaged could not be repaired, as the rise and fall of tide was never more than nine feet, while the draft of water was nineteen feet, and as for heaving a ship down among ice when she has been damaged, that is a vain attempt. The fourth, and indeed great reason why Sir John Franklin's expedition has not been heard of since 23rd July, 1845, is that he had no vessel of retreat, a circumstance which, after the experience of my last voyage, in which our safety under Divine Providence is to be attributed to our having a *dépôt* of provisions and boats sufficient to save the crews at a distance to which we could retreat, was not to be lost sight of. His Lordship referring to my plan of four small vessels equal to carry the same quantity of provisions as two large ones—one to be a steamer, and another a vessel of retreat, which would secure a return in case of accident, seemed to incline to my opinion; but unfortunately the Council consisted of those who were adverse to my proposal or to any proposal which emanated from me ; and the answer I received, after a month's delay, was, as before stated.

Thus the favourable season presenting a most important opportunity, which, properly used by adopting the measures I had suggested, and which would have certainly led to results conclusive, probably favourable to the cause of humanity and science, was most wantonly lost, and no small weight of responsibility rests both upon the Board of Admiralty and Royal Society for the prominent part they respectively took in this most unfortunate misapprehension of duty. The Astronomical Society, to which I also applied, was favourable, and decided that if the Royal Society gave their recommendation, the President and Council of the Astronomical Society would back the recommendation, which of course fell to the ground, but which was not to be wondered at, as some were members of both societies.

Although I had not been invited to any of the consultations held on the subject of Sir John Franklin's expedition, either touching the equipment, prospects, or position of his ships; and although my opinions, especially that he would not succeed, were held in contempt and derision, I considered it a duty I owed to my friend, who had been so sincere and active in my rescue, to communicate with his amiable and talented Lady, and for this purpose I called at her residence, Bedford-place, and saw her father.

Her Ladyship being at Brighton, I offered to go there to see her, and of this she was informed. But she, too, had been cajoled! "Sir John Ross," she was informed, "is the only one who says Sir John Franklin cannot succeed—and at any rate, he can easily get to the whalers—Sir John Ross's plans are all absurd." And I was given to understand that her Ladyship was indignant that I should throw any doubt on the subject. Her father never returned my call, and my offer not being accepted, I could not proceed further in that direction; which I deeply regret, as I am confident I could have convinced her that no time was to be lost, and even if I was in error, it was on the safe side; that my plan of four small instead of two large vessels would extend the search, and that if the expedition was frozen up (as probably the case) Sir John had neither a *dépôt* nor a vessel of retreat, or boats belonging to the ship that could carry half his crew, or even if they had such boats they could not be converted to the use by being carried over the ice, as proved by my being obliged to abandon such boats halfway on my last expedition.

The following paper was submitted to the consideration of the British Association for the Advancement of Science, on the expedition under the command of Sir John Franklin—Oxford, 23rd June, 1847.

As the interest in the discovery of the north-west passage had been lying dormant after Parry's failure in 1825 had been revived by me in 1829, and, since my return in 1833, has occupied a considerable share in the attention of the public ; and as the anxiety for the fate of the ships now employed in that arduous service has increased by the certainty that they cannot have succeeded, as was expected during the last autumn, either in accomplishing the desired object or in returning to England ; and it is known that I had promised Sir John Franklin, who took great interest in my rescue, that in return I would volunteer my services, in search of him and his brave companions ; I have thought it would be satisfactory to the British Association for the Advancement of Science that I should briefly state my opinion as to the probability of his present situation and prospect of success, but more particularly to describe the disadvantages under which he labours—a task which it shall be one of my objects to perform, and which is the more readily undertaken inasmuch as it may, on the one hand, prepare the public to be more liberal in their praise, should his efforts prove ultimately successful, and, on the other hand, should the difficulties that beset him be too great for him to overcome, to withhold that censure which is too oft visited on those who unfortunately fail to gratify the highly wrought expectations of the public.

Sir John Barrow, who (notwithstanding the undeniable opposition of Dr. Scoresby) in his published autobiography, still persists that he was the originator of the expedition of 1818, is without doubt entitled to be styled the promoter of that now commanded by Sir John Franklin, and as such must be considered as obnoxious to the observations I have to make on this undertaking. In the first place, I shall observe, that from the loss of the *Fury*, and the danger to which the *Hecla* was exposed, from their great draft of water, he must have been fully aware of that great disadvantage ; is it not, therefore, extraordinary that he should have fixed on two ships still larger than those mentioned, and of a greater draft of water ? It was well known that field ice in that region was twelve feet thick, but the *Erebus* and *Terror* drew nineteen feet or more. The ships when beset are in a helpless state, carried along by the ice, wherever it is impelled by wind, tide, or current, and should they be drifted in this state over a shoal or bed of rocks, above which the ice would float but not the ships, their loss would be inevitable, and the unfortunate crews cast upon the ice in a state of destitution! This might, and, I will add, ought to have been avoided, and great expense saved also, by choosing vessels of a draft of water less than ten feet, which would carry, in proportion to the crews, an equal quantity of provisions, should this accident have happened, and if they were reduced to their own exertions for a supply of food, their misery would be much aggravated by their number (138) to be provided for. And even if only one of the two vessels has been lost, this will throw both crews on the other, and thus they may be by this time in distress ! The next disadvantage I shall mention is the inexperience of the officers and crews in the navigation of those seas, for, excepting Captain Crozier and the two ice-masters, there are none who have had any practice in that peculiar kind of navigation. The screw propeller might be of service until they were beset in the ice, after that it could be of no use whatever, while it must be admitted that the part of the ship where the screw is fitted must be materially weakened, and less able to sustain the pressure to which it would be occasionally exposed. It must be recollected that Sir John Franklin was to try what his predecessor Parry and the majority of his officers considered imprudent, to put the ships into the ice, either in the Wellington Channel or at the west end of Melville Island, and run the risk of being able to make his way through the ice to Behring's Strait. It is probable, indeed, if he gets so far, that when he and his officers saw the consequence of doing what Parry thought so imprudent, that he deemed it proper to wait an opportunity, when the sea to the westward of Melville Island appeared favourable, and make a push in the direct course. But, as I have already said, he cannot have succeeded in getting through during last autumn, or we must have heard long since of his arrival at the Sandwich Islands, Kamtschatka, or Panama; and as the whalers of last season (1846) have reported that Lancaster Sound was unnavigable and full of ice, he could not have returned had he desired it. It is true the ships cannot be said to be missing, as they had provisions (if no accident had happened to either) until the summer of 1848. Sir John Richardson has been directed by Government to prepare a quantity of provisions to be sent through the Hudson's Bay Company to the northern coast of America, in case the ships should have to pass another winter there, or in having been obliged to abandon them, to make the best of their way to the possessions of the Hudson's Bay Company, near the mouth of the Mackenzie River; however, sanguine hopes may still be entertained not only of their safety but success. Nor would it be at all surprising or alarming if the expedition is not heard of, in either October or in January next, because the reports from Canada and Sweden represent the last winter as having been uncommonly severe and long; and in the event of the ships being frozen up, as my vessel was, no relief can arrive at them by sea until August, 1848. In the event of the expedition not being heard of in February, I have no doubt that an expedition of relief by sea will be sent out in June, 1848, which, in my opinion, will be most likely to accomplish the rescue, should an accident have happened, or to supply them with provisions.

I have annexed to this paper a small scale, which in the first place points out the position of the ships when last seen; secondly, where it is probable either would be left if they advanced, and possibly provisions would be deposited; and lastly, the position near Cornwallis Island where they would most likely be frozen up, should they not make their appearance on the other side.

Appended to this paper was my plan of four vessels, already given.

The following answer was received by me from D. S. Ansted, Secretary to C Section, British Association:—

Committee Rooms, Section C, Oxford, June 24, 1847.

SIR,

I have the honour to inform you that your paper on "The Expedition under the command of Sir John Franklin," was this day considered by the Committee of Section C, to which it was referred by the Assistant General Secretary, and that the Committee passed the following resolution : "Resolved, that the paper of Sir John Ross be declined, it being contrary to the objects of the British Association to discuss the propriety of an expedition undertaken by Government."

I have the honour to be,

Your obedient servant,

D. S. ANSTED, Sec. to Section C.

To Sir John Ross.

By this decision I was denied the privilege of discussion, nor was questioned on the subject, although it was notorious that, previous to Sir John Franklin's departure, and at every subsequent meeting but this at Oxford, the Association not only interfered, but gave strong recommendations in favour of succeeding expeditions. A proposal of Dr. Lee, recommending my plan of measuring an arc of the meridian at Spitzbergen, met the same fate from this untoward committee.

As time wore on, it was with heartfelt grief I observed that, as usual after a very mild season, that which succeeded was severe ; and it was with mixed feelings of hope and anxiety I looked for the return of my gallant friend, or that news would be heard of his having passed Behring's Straits ; but the month of November, 1847, put an end to the hope of his return, and the probability was that, having wintered somewhere in Barrow's Strait, owing to the mildness of the preceding winter of 1846-7, the ice had opened, and, taking advantage of this illusory circumstance, he was induced to push on, in hopes of complete success, and, consequently, had been frozen in either between Bank's Land and Cape Walker, or, having tried the Wellington Channel, he was beset at the north of the North Georgian Islands. The opposite party then took the alarm, for the arrival of Dr. Rae, confirming all my assertions respecting a passage south of Boothia were found to be correct, and the assertion of any passage in that direction was clearly a palpable fabrication to injure my professional reputation, and the object of my opponents was now turned of course to frustrate my endeavours to command the expedition, which it was now evident must be fitted out for the next season. Accordingly, unknown to me, a meeting was held at Lady Franklin's residence, at which all my proposals were sneered at and my opinions scouted, while I was represented to be too old and infirm to undertake such a service; and the objections of my nephew's wife's friends and his own being removed, it was agreed that Lady Franklin should write to Lord Auckland, to request that his Lordship would give the command of the expedition to him instead of to me. This information was given to me by a friend who was present, and who requested his name should not be mentioned. But I did not receive this information until after I had written the following letter to the Secretary, applying for the command, and enclosing a plan for a new expedition of four vessels; for although I was confident that the favourable season had passed and been lost, and that the prospect before us was anything but cheering, still, further delay was out of the question; and I was certain that, under existing circumstances, small vessels such as I recommended were the most efficient.

16, Park-street, Grosvenor-square, Nov. 13, 1847.

SIR,
      Herewith you will receive, for the information of the Right Honourable the Earl of Auckland, the following statement touching the progress, difficulties, and probable position of the expedition for the discovery of a north-west passage, under the command of Sir John Franklin, together with the inclosed plan, being a proposal which, in my humble opinion, is not only the most efficient for the rescue of that gallant officer and those under his command, but also provides with certainty for the safe return of those employed in this interesting and arduous service. First, touching the circumstances under which Sir John Franklin left this country in May, 1845. The success and progress of an expedition which has to navigate Baffin's Bay and the seas to the westward, depend much on the mildness or the severity of the winter that preceded its departure, and that of 1844-5 being more than usually severe, the progress made, by accounts from the whalers, was fourteen days later, in crossing to the west land, in that season, than usual; therefore Cornwallis Island is certainly the furthest that could be accomplished by the expedition in 1845.

The winter of 1846 having been more mild, there can be no doubt that the attempt would be made to make the passage, when consequently an opportunity offered. By the last letters received from Mr. Reid, the master of the *Erebus*, it was his advice that the expedition should keep well to the northward, until they reached the longitude of Behring's Strait, and then "bear up." But as no accounts have been received of the expedition during 1847, it is evident the ships have not succeeded in the autumn of 1846 in passing Behring's Strait, the ships must, therefore, be frozen up, either among the ice or in some harbour, if they have not suffered shipwreck. Now as the winter of 1845-6 was not only more severe but three weeks longer than usual, there can be no doubt they would be under the necessity of continuing in their position, and that they could not be extricated, even if they had met with no damage, until August, 1847, at least; and, as they have not returned by way of Baffin's Bay, they cannot be heard of in the Pacific until the end of January, 1848.

2dly. Touching the "difficulties and disadvantages under which he labours." The first I shall allude to is the size and consequent great draught of water of the two ships—namely, nineteen feet. This is a very great disadvantage, as when the ships are beset with field-ice, as must unavoidably be the case, after passing the west-end of Melville Island, which ice is only ten feet thick, if carried over shoals or rocks, the ships will take the ground before the ice, and, as was the case with the *Fury*, be inevitably lost. The *Victory* (my vessel) drew only seven feet, and as the ice always grounded first, she met with no damage, but the rocks which she passed over were often seen under her bottom. Besides, in the event of damage, the bottom of a ship, drawing nineteen feet water, cannot be repaired by laying her on the ground, when the tide, as is the case in these regions, only recedes eight or nine feet. The second disadvantage is, that only two of the crew in each ship have ever navigated among ice, Sir John Franklin not having taken the precaution of securing men used to that kind of navigation, to the use of ice anchors, ice saws, and the appearance of danger from the mast-head. Ships of a large size are also in proportion much more difficult to manage among ice, and much less able to withstand the pressure of the ice when beset; finally, the difficulty of providing for so many men in the event of the ship being abandoned.

3rdly. Touching the various plans proposed. That under the direction of Sir John Richardson cannot be of any use in extricating them from their present position, and can only be considered as useful in carrying a supply to the Mackenzie River establishment, for their use, if ever they reach it. If the crews of the ships are obliged to abandon them or their position, they must do so in the month of April next, and if the Mackenzie River is their destination, they would arrive (if they *arrived at all*) before the end of June; after which time it is impossible for Sir John Richardson's party to proceed to look for them, or for either party to travel over rough and broken ice, on which the snow has melted. His party must, therefore, winter at the Mackenzie, and proceed in the spring of 1849, when it would be too late to find any of them alive!

4thly. Touching Dr. King's plan. Were the objects only to inform Sir John Franklin that a ship had been sent to the north-west corner of North Somerset, he would no doubt have a better chance of finding him, *viâ* Coppermine River, than Dr. Richardson. But this information he already possesses from me, before he left England, and as Dr. King cannot pretend to carry any provisions more than necessary for the support of his own party, he could bring them no relief, and therefore his journey would be of little service, excepting as a guide. And as Sir John Franklin is also aware that he will find cruisers, if fortunate enough to pass Behring's Straits, nothing further need be said on that subject.*

5thly. Touching the probability of their present position. Admitting, in the first place, that neither ship has been wrecked, as the winds and currents (which are always influenced by the winds) are, both by Sir E. Parry's accounts and mine, in the proportion of 2 to 1 from the north-westward, the ships must, after they had passed Melville Island, have been carried in the opposite direction; and the probability is, that they are either at Bank's Land of Parry or between that and the west side of Boothia Felix, and certainly from 400 to 600 miles from the northern coast of America, which, especially if they had to travel over land, would be impossible; and I cannot believe that it would be attempted. It must be remembered that the *Victory's* men, who had to travel scarcely half the distance, were obliged to abandon our boats after the first week of our journey, and arrived at Fury Beach completely exhausted, on the 1st of July, at which time the ice became suddenly covered with water by the melting of the snow. If, as was their first intention, the expedition passed to the northward by the Wellington Channel, their situation is still more critical, and totally beyond the power of either Sir John Richardson or Dr. King to reach their position, or afford any relief. Indeed, I may safely assert that Sir John Franklin can have no hope but in the plan which I have recommended, and of which I made him aware before he sailed ; and if one of the ships has been wrecked—a circumstance not at all improbable—and the crews of both subsisting on the provisions of the other, their situation must be already deplorable ;

* If Dr. King had fortunately discovered Sir John Franklin, which is probable, he would, at any rate, have rendered subsequent search unnecessary.

and it was principally on that account I volunteered to proceed to their relief during the last summer.

I trust, sir, that when the Earl of Auckland has taken into consideration the kind interest which his late Majesty's Government, and particularly Sir John Franklin, took on my account, when in a similar situation, his Lordship's candour will view my anxiety with allowance, excuse my zeal, and pardon this trespass on his Lordship's attention.

I have the honour to be, sir,

Your most obedient, humble servant,

JOHN ROSS, Captain, R.N.

To this letter the usual reply was made,—" that it had been received and laid before their Lordships,"—but no other steps were taken.

Time fleeted on. Thus repulsed and embarrassed by the frigid treatment of the Admiralty, the stupid pertinacity which guided or restrained the Councils of the Royal and other Societies, which extended to the British Association for the Advancement of Science, I made every possible exertion to raise funds among my friends in order to fit out a private expedition in search of Sir John Franklin ; but in vain. I would, indeed, willingly have done so at my own expense, convinced that the fate of my valued friend, who had taken such deep interest in my own rescue, depended on the efforts that ought to be made in a season so favourable for the undertaking; but I had re-cently met with severe pecuniary losses, which put the attainment of this fondly-cherished object totally out of my power.

In November, 1847, it appears that a meeting was held at the house of Lady Franklin, consisting of those who had opposed my propositions above-mentioned, and from which I was of course excluded; and being unacquainted with the proceedings of this assembly of Arctic *Savans*, and it being now admitted by the public that the time had at length arrived, when search should be made, I again tendered my services, with my plan of four vessels as before detailed; and was received by Lord Auckland, then First Lord of the Admiralty, with every encouragement, his Lordship not only permitting me to hope that I might have command of the searching expedition, according to my own plan, but showing his regret that my former offer had been rejected. In the mean time I went to my residence in Scotland, to settle my private affairs, under the expectation of employment in the spring of 1848, and having returned to London I was not long kept in suspense. Lord Auckland sent for me, and informed me that he had received a letter from Lady Franklin, requesting him to appoint my nephew, Sir James Clark Ross, to command the expedition instead of me! I replied to his Lordship that I was happy to hear it, that he was a clever young man, but he did not volunteer to look for Sir John before he sailed; and I understood that he had declined the command, in consequence of a promise to his wife's family, that he would not go to sea any more. His Lordship then added, " He disapproves of your plan of four small vessels," which he then returned to me, and said that two large ships are already in progress for him. Besides the known opposition he always made to any plan of mine, it could not but be evident to me that the north-west passage was his main object, and especially to prevent me from obtaining it, he had got the permission of the family to " stand in my shoes." And I replied to this decision, by saying, emphatically, that " He cannot intend to search for Franklin!" having many times heard him declare, " how much better small ships were than large ones." But I immediately saw through his intention, which could be no other than the survey of the western coasts of North Somerset and Boothia, and thereby determine the north-west passage. I therefore replied,—" My Lord, Sir James Ross can have no intention of searching for Sir John Franklin; he knows better than to trust himself in such ships to follow the track of Franklin. His object is the north-west passage, by surveying the western coasts of North Somerset and Boothia." His Lordship seemed not a little confounded at this remark, but said— " I shall take care of that, and order him to the north shore of Barrow's Strait, and his second in command to navigate the western shore of North Somerset." But the decision was already made; two ships, utterly unfit for such a service, were purchased and fitted out at nearly double the expense of my plan of four small vessels.

There can be no doubt that Sir J. C. Ross and his friend Sir John Barrow had made up their minds to treat the search for poor Franklin as a secondary consideration, in order to accomplish their favourite object, the north-west passage, consoling themselves with the idea that he would make for the American Continent, and that Richardson and Rae would get hold of him and his companions; and it will be seen that notwithstanding (as Lord Auckland told me) Sir J. C. Ross's orders were to keep the north shore and proceed towards Melville Island, while Captain Bird, second in command, was to winter on the north side of North Somerset, and survey its coast, Sir James Ross, as I had anticipated, found an excuse to occupy the ground laid out for Captain Bird (from whom he kept the orders secret), in direct violation of the Admiralty Instructions!

In the meantime two ships were purchased, one from Messrs. Wigram for £17,370, the other from Messrs. Green for £15,750; while the whole four small vessels, which would carry the same quantity of provisions, would cost, completely fitted, £2000 each, and with fewer men to navigate them, the cost would not be half what one of the two large ships would amount to in a voyage of thirteen months, whilst it must be admitted that the search would be materially extended. But, on the other hand, there would be less patronage, a consideration that is always kept in view in every *job* of the kind.

To add to the absurdity of all these proceedings, the *Plover*, a ship that was known to be a "*beast of burden*," and a very bad sailer, was selected for the long voyage to Behring's Straits, and did not leave England until January, 1848, and of course could not get to Behring's Straits that year, and was obliged to winter on the coast of Siberia, to the south-east of the Straits. But the most absurd of all the expeditions was that of Sir John Richardson, whom I heard bragging in the Royal Society that he would find Sir John Franklin; and at that august assembly I suffered the usual amount of abuse for *daring* to doubt his success, while I could not in any way discover that, even if he did find Franklin and his companions, he could have afforded them the smallest relief!

The individuals most to be pitied on this occasion were the amiable lady and daughter of Sir John Franklin, whose minds had been deceived by the unworthy conduct of her advisers. I saw the time would come when it would be but too obvious that my opinions ought not to have been disregarded, or my proposals rejected with scorn, while my calls on her ladyship's aged father remained unnoticed, and my offers of communication were unanswered.

The Earl of Auckland informed me that Sir J. C. Ross had a *carte blanche* touching the equipment of the vessels he had chosen, and also the nomination of his second in command and other officers. He selected, therefore, Captain Bird, who had obtained his promotion by being with him in the Antarctic Expedition; a person most suitable to answer his purpose, and from whom he could more easily conceal his views. The ships were named the *Enterprise* and *Investigator*. Sufficiently, indeed, indicative of the *double* service they had to perform, but, especially without a small vessel of retreat, totally useless for the relief of Sir John Franklin and his companions. Each ship was supplied with a steam launch, which it was not doubted would materially assist in the navigation of Baffin's Bay and examination of Barrow's Strait; but it will be seen that they never were applied to any such service, but intended for one totally different. The *Enterprise* was 470 and *Investigator* 420 tons, having each seventy men; and when they left Gravesend, on the 12th of May, 1848, the former drew nineteen and the latter eighteen feet of water, which at once confirmed my suspicion, that the search for the missing expedition was a *blind*, or a secondary object. The following are the Admiralty Instructions to Sir J. C. Ross:—

By the Commissioners for executing the office of Lord High Admiral, &c.

Whereas the period for which the ships *Erebus* and *Terror* were victualled will terminate at the end of this summer, and whereas no tidings whatever of the proceedings of either of these ships have reached us since their first entry into Lancaster Sound, in the year 1845, and there being therefore reason to apprehend that they have been blocked up by immovable ice, and they may soon be exposed to suffer great privation; we have deemed it no longer proper to defer to endeavour to afford them adequate relief. Having therefore caused to be prepared and duly equipped with extra stores and provisions two suitable vessels, having had them properly fortified so as to resist the pressure of the ice, and having the fullest confidence in the skill and experience you have acquired in

D

these inclement seas, we have thought proper to place them under your command; and you are hereby required and directed, as soon as they are in all respects ready for sea, to proceed in the *Enterprise*, under your immediate command, and taking the *Investigator* (Captain Bird) under your orders, without delay to Lancaster Sound. In your progress through that inlet to the westward, you will carefully search both shores, as well as those of narrow straits, for any notice that may have been deposited there, or for the casual indications of their having been visited by any of Sir John Franklin's ships.

Should your early arrival there, or the fortunately protracted openness of the season, admit of your at once extending a similar examination to the shores of the Wellington Channel, it will leave you at greater liberty to devote yourself more fully afterwards to your researches to the westward. The several intervals of coast that appear in our charts to lie between Capes Clarence and Walker must next be carefully explored, and as each of your vessels have been furnished with a launch fitted with a small engine and screw capable of propelling it between four and five knots, we trust by their means, or by the ships' boats, all those preliminary researches may be completed during the present season, and consequently before it may be necessary to secure the ships for the winter. As that winter may possibly prove to be so severe as to seal up the western end of that extensive inlet, and as it would be unwise to allow both vessels to be set there, we consider that it would be prudent to look out for a fit and safe part near Cape Rennell, and in that neighbourhood, to secure the *Investigator* for the ensuing winter. From that position a considerable extent of coast may be explored on foot, and in the following spring detached parties may be sent across the ice by Captain Bird, in order to look thoroughly into the creeks along the western coast of Boothia, and even as far as Cape Nicolai ; while another party may proceed to the southward, and ascertain whether the blank space shown there in our charts consists of an open sea, through which Sir John Franklin may have passed, or, on the contrary, a continuous chain of islands, among which he may still be blocked up. As soon as the returning summer shall have opened a passage between the land and the main body of the ice, this eastern vessel is to detach her steam launch to Lancaster Sound, in order to meet the whale ships which usually visit the western side of Baffin's Bay about that time, and by which we propose to send out further instructions and communications to you, as well as to receive in return an account of your proceedings.

The *Enterprise*, in the meantime, will press forward to the westward, and endeavour to reach Winter Harbour in Melville Island, or perhaps, if circumstances should in your judgment render it desirable, to push or bear to Banks's Land; but in either case a distinct statement of the measures you are going to adopt, as well as of your future intentions, should be deposited in some spot previously communicated to Captain Bird. From this western station you will be able to spread some active parties, to make some short and useful excursions before the season altogether closes, and still more effective ones in the ensuing spring; one party should then pursue the coast in whatever direction it may seem likely to have been followed by Sir John Franklin, and thus determine the general shape of Banks's Land. It is then to proceed to Cape Bathurst or to Cape Parry on the main land, at each of which places we have directed Sir John Richardson to leave provisions for its use; that party will then advance to Fort Good Hope, where they will find directions for continuing their progress up the Mackenzie River, so as to return to England by the route of traders.

Another party will explore the eastern coast of Banks's Land, and from thence make at once for Cape Krusenstern, where, or at Cape Hearne, a *caché* of pemmican will be placed for Sir John Richardson.

They should communicate immediately with him, according to the agreement which he and you may have made; and placing themselves under his orders, they will assist him in examining the shores of Victoria and Wollaston Islands."

The expedition under Captain Sir James Clark Ross, consisting of the *Enterprise*, of 540 tons, commanded by himself, and the *Investigator*, Captain Bird, under his orders, provisioned for three years, sailed on the 18th June, 1848, furnished with steam launches (which, however, were never used during the voyage), and accompanied by a transport to make up the expenditure of provisions at Disco or Whale Fish Islands; and as I predicted, the season, from the severity of the preceding winter, was unfavourable for navigation, and the two ships, instead of proceeding according to the Admiralty orders, had barely time to slip into the snug harbour named after Prince Leopold, where they were destined to enjoy themselves for eleven months. Parties were indeed sent out in different directions, but none to Cape Walker, or any part mentioned in the instructions. The attempt to solve the question of the north-west passage by surveying the west coast of Boothia, which appears to have been the grand object, was a complete failure; and, compared with the feats performed by the officers and men of the subsequent expeditions, they fall miserably below par. But although Sir J. C. Ross failed in finding any of the missing crews, which most undoubtedly he would have done had he persevered, and although he did not accomplish the grand object of the north-west passage, he succeeded, by being frozen in for eleven months in a comfortable ship's cabin, in serving his *sea* time, which, according to the regulations of the service, entitled him to his flag on the *active* list when he came by seniority for promotion. Being, of course, unable to send one ship home without risking the loss of the other, he returned to England with both ships: after being for twenty-four days beset in the middle of the pack, and drifted helplessly out of Lancaster Sound, the ships were "miraculously released," and reached England on the 5th of November, to excite universal disappointment.

It was not until the return of Sir James Clark Ross's expedition, in 1849, which was a complete failure, that I learnt extracts from my letter to Sir Charles Adam had been submitted to Sir Edward Parry and others, a revelation which had been brought to light by a motion in the House of Commons by Sir Robert Inglis. But although extracts of this letter were treated as an official correspondence, the entire letter appears to have been considered private, as it was not included in the returns moved for. And, in comparison with the extracts, the real meaning of my letter has, whether wilfully or by mistake I shall not seek to determine, been unwarrantably misconstrued ; and if the Reports of Sir Edward Parry, Sir J. C. Ross, Colonel Sabine, and others, had been referred to me, as I submit they ought to have been, the misconstruction put on my letters, or rather extracts from my letters, would have been forthwith explained. However, even in the imperfect state in which my letter was brought before the public, no one could justly put such a construction on my words as appears to have been given to them both by the Admiralty and the individuals called upon for their Report.

Proposed Plans for Relief of the Arctic Expedition.

Admiralty, Feb. 19, 1847.

SIR,

I am commanded by my Lords Commissioners of the Admiralty to transmit to you the enclosed extracts of two recent letters from Captain Sir John Ross, and to request that you will favour them with the substance of any communication which Sir John Franklin, before his departure from England, may have made to you with regard to his expectations and intentions that depôts should be formed at certain places for his relief (no record of such intentions or expectations having been left on record here), their Lordships being sure that, from his known intimacy with you, he would either have consulted you on the subject, or communicated to you his intentions.

I am further desired to mention to you, that their Lordships, having unlimited confidence in the skill and resources of Sir John Franklin, have as yet felt no apprehensions about his safety; but, on the other hand, it is obvious, that if no accounts of him should arrive by the end of this year, or, as Sir John Ross expects, at an earlier period, active steps must be then taken.

I am therefore commanded to call upon you for your opinions on the subject, both with respect to the question of employing vessels, the period of their sailing, and the several places which it would be expedient to visit, as well as for any advice which may occur to you, who have had so much personal experience of the Arctic Regions, and whose feelings must be so deeply engaged in the hazardous enterprise of those most valuable officers and men; and it would be satisfactory to their Lordships if you would call upon Sir James Ross, Colonel Sabine, and Sir John Richardson, to enter into consultations with you.

(Signed)   W. A. B. HAMILTON.

Captain Sir Edward Parry.

(Captain Sir James Ross.
Colonel Sabine.
Sir John Richardson.)

Extracts of Letters alluded to from Captain Sir John Ross.

16, Park-street, Grosvenor-square,
London, Jan. 27, 1847.

SIR,

In reference to the several communications I have made to my Lords Commissioners of the Admiralty, touching the probable position of the discovery ships under the command of Sir John Franklin, and in the performance of a promise I made to that gallant officer, namely, that if no accounts were received from him up to the middle of January, 1847, I would volunteer my services to ascertain his fate, and to visit the several depôts we had fixed before his departure from England :

I beg most respectfully to state, for the information of my Lords Commissioners of the Admiralty, that my opinion, founded on my experience in the Arctic regions, and on my knowledge of the intentions of Sir John Franklin, is, in the first place, that he cannot have succeeded in passing through Behring's Straits, because the expedition, had it been successful, would have been heard of before the middle of this month; and, in the second place, the probability is, that his ships have been carried by drift ice into a position from which they cannot be extricated.

16, Park-street, Grosvenor-square,
London, Feb. 9, 1847.

Sir,

In reference to the communication I had the honour of making to you this morning, when I pointed out the impossibility of Sir John Franklin and his crew being able to reach the nearest place a whaling ship could be found, from the position in which the expedition must be frozen up, consequent on the known intentions of Sir John Franklin to put his ships into the drift ice at the western end of Melville Island,—a risk which was deemed in the highest degree imprudent by Lieutenant Parry and the officers of the expedition of 1819-20, with ships of a less draft of water, and in every respect better calculated to sustain the pressure of the ice, and other dangers to which they must be exposed;—and as it is now evident that the expedition cannot have succeeded in passing Behring's Straits, and, if not totally lost, must have been carried by the ice known to drift to the southward, on land seen at a great distance in that direction, and from which the accumulation of ice behind them will, as in my own case, for ever prevent the return of the ships : they must be abandoned, either on the 1st of May next, in order to reach Melville Island before the snow melts, at the end of June, and where they must remain until the 1st of August, and at which place I had selected to leave a depôt of provisions, absolutely necessary for their sustenance, or if they defer their journey until the 1st of May, 1848, it will be still more necessary that provisions, fuel, &c., should be deposited there : after I had secured my vessel in a harbour on the south side of Barrow's Strait, and in such a position as would enable them to reach her when the sea was sufficiently open for boats, which I would leave at the depôt in " Winter Harbour," while in the meantime I would survey the west coast of Boothia, and in all probability decide the question of a north-west passage. I was officially acquainted by Captain Hamilton that it was the intention of their Lordships not to accede to my proposal, but to offer a reward to whalers, and to the Hudson's Bay Company, to use their endeavours for the rescue of Sir John Franklin and his companions, a proposition I hereby protest against as utterly inefficient; for as one of the officers of Parry's expedition, who was then of opinion that what Sir John Franklin intended to do was imprudent, and who from experience knew with what extreme difficulty we travelled 300 miles over much smoother ice after we abandoned our vessel, it must be certain that Franklin and his men, 138 in number, could not possibly travel 600 miles; again, we had in prospect the *Fury's* stores to sustain us after our arrival, besides boats, and unless I reach Melville Island while summer, they will have nothing.

I have, &c.

(Signed)   JOHN ROSS, Captain, R.N.

Reply from Sir Edward Parry to the Extracts of Sir John Ross's Letter.

Haslar Hospital, Gosport, Feb. 23, 1847.

SIR,

With reference to your communication of the 19th instant, on the subject of the Polar Expedition under the orders of Captain Sir John Franklin, I have the honour to acquaint you, for the information of my Lords Commissioners of the Admiralty, that on the receipt of your letter I wrote to Captain Sir James C. Ross and Colonel Sabine respectively, suggesting to them, as the only practicable mode of communication between us, that they should favour me in writing with their views on the several points to which our attention has been directed. With Sir John Richardson I have had the advantage of being able fully to discuss the whole question ; and, pending the receipt of the replies from the other two officers, I beg to submit the following remarks as the result of my own mature deliberation upon the subject.

As to any communication which Sir John Franklin had with me before he left England with regard to his expectations and intentions that depôts should be formed at certain places for his relief, I have no recollection whatever of any such communication, which could scarcely have escaped my memory had it ever occurred ; and I venture to add, that had any idea of this kind seriously suggested itself to Sir John Franklin's mind, he could not have failed to make it the subject of an official representation to the Admiralty, as the only correct or practicable channel through which he could expect to carry out an intention of this nature.

The conclusions at which their Lordships have arrived, both as to the absence of any present cause for apprehension, and the expediency of using active measures, should no intelligence of the expedition reach England within a reasonable period, exactly coincide with my own.

Former experience has clearly shown, that, with the resources taken from this country, two winters may be passed in the Polar regions, not only in safety, but with comfort;* and if any inference can be drawn from the absence of all intelligence of the expedition up to this time, I am disposed to consider it rather in favour than otherwise of the success which has attended their efforts.

I conceive, however, that the time has arrived when due preparation should be made for instituting, if necessary, an active search for the ships, and conveying supplies to their crews, in case no information should be received respecting them in the autumn of the present year.

In considering the measures to be pursued for this purpose, I am strongly of opinion that it would be attended with very little probability of success, while it would involve great expense for the Government, to send other ships of their own in quest of the expedition. No vessel could safely be dispatched on this service without being strengthened, and otherwise efficiently equipped both for navigating and wintering among the ice ; and even then, the search could not prudently be made with the requisite energy and perseverance by any single vessel : in my opinion, nothing short of a second well-equipped expedition could be expected to do more than penetrate through Barrow's Strait, as high as Prince Regent's Inlet, which may be considered as the mere threshold of the enterprise in which the *Erebus* and *Terror* are engaged.

Up to that point, however, which is not uncommonly attained by the whalers, I believe that information might just as probably be obtained by offering to those ships a reasonable premium either for procuring authentic information of the expedition, or for rendering them any assistance. This they might possibly do, to a certain extent, so far as information is concerned, by looking out, in prominent positions, for the piles of stones and flag-staves under which in former expeditions it has been customary to bury bottles or copper cylinders containing some account of their proceedings. I do not think that anything further can be done by ships, except at a heavy expense, and virtually involving the exposure of a second expedition to the risks inseparable from such an enterprise.

The only plan which appears to me to hold out a reasonable prospect of success, is by making an effort to push supplies to the

* At this time the discovery of the defective character of the preserved meats supplied to Sir John Franklin had not been made.

northern coast of the American Continent, and the islands adjacent thereto, with the assistance of the Hudson's Bay Company, and by the modes of travelling in ordinary use among their servants. As the experience of Sir John Richardson in such enterprises, in which he has already borne so honourable and distinguished a part, renders him peculiarly competent to offer advice on all matters of detail relating to this subject, I beg leave to refer their Lordships to his letter, herewith enclosed, in which he suggests the propriety of immediate steps being taken, in concert with the Hudson's Bay Company, by way of preparation for what it may be necessary to do when the time for action arrives, that is, in case no intelligence of the expedition shall have arrived before the close of the present year.

Upon the plan which Sir John Richardson proposes, I will only remark that nothing less effective than what he suggests can be available for the relief of the crews (supposing them to require it, under the contingencies to which he alludes), though simpler means of the same kind might be effectual for merely obtaining information respecting them.

I beg, in conclusion, to add, that it might be likewise satisfactory to their Lordships (as suggested by Sir John Barrow) to adopt at the same time the only remaining mode of obtaining information of the expedition, namely, to direct the Commander-in-chief in the Pacific to send a small vessel to look into Behring's Straits, and, if practicable, to dispatch a boat along the shore of the American Continent to the eastward, in the manner pursued by Captain Beechey in the *Blossom*, when endeavouring to meet the former expedition under Sir John Franklin.

I have, &c.

(Signed)   W. E. PARRY, Captain.

P.S.—27 February.   Not having received the expected replies from Captain Sir James C. Ross or Colonel Sabine, I consider it expedient to transmit my own communication and that of Sir John Richardson without further delay.

Reply of Sir John Richardson to the Extracts of Sir John Ross's Letter.

Haslar Hospital, Feb. 25, 1847.

SIR,

Having been furnished, by directions of my Lords Commissioners of the Admiralty, with extracts from Sir John Ross's letters, relating to the expedition under command of Sir John Franklin, and also with a copy of their Lordships' letter to you on the same subject, I beg leave to offer the following observations for your consideration.

I had many conversations with Sir John Franklin, up to the eve of his departure, respecting his future proceedings, and also received a communication from him written on the coast of Greenland, but never heard him express a wish or expectation of depôts of provisions being stored for him on Melville Island or elsewhere, and knowing him, as I do most intimately, I must express my belief that he would have preferred such a request to the Government alone.

Reply from Captain Sir James C. Ross to the Extract of Sir John Ross's Letter.

Aston House, Aylesbury, March 2, 1847.

MY DEAR SIR EDWARD,

In reply to your letter of the 22nd February, I have to inform you that I do not think there is the smallest reason of apprehension or anxiety for the safety and success of the expedition under the command of Sir John Franklin; no one acquainted with the nature of the navigation of the Polar Sea would have expected they would have been able to get through to Behring's Straits without spending at least two winters in those regions, except under unusually favourable circumstances, which all the accounts from the whalers concur in proving they have not experienced, and I am quite sure neither Sir John Franklin nor Captain Crozier expected to do so.

Their last letters to me from Whalefish Islands, the day previous to their departure from them, inform me that they had taken on board provisions for three years on full allowance, which they could extend to four years without any serious inconvenience; so that we may feel assured they cannot want from that cause until after the middle of July, 1849; it therefore does not appear to me at all desirable to send after them until the spring of the next year.

With reference to that part of Mr. Ward's letter respecting Sir John Franklin's expectations of *depôts* of provisions being formed at certain places, I can very confidently assert that no expectation of the kind was seriously entertained by him; Captain Crozier was staying with me at Blackheath nearly all the time the expedition was fitting out, and with Sir John Franklin I was in almost daily and unreserved communication respecting the details of the equipment and future proceedings of the expedition, and neither of them made the least allusion to any such arrangements or expectations, beyond mentioning as an absurdity what Sir John Ross had proposed to Sir John Franklin.

In reply to the question you propose to me, as to the proper steps to be pursued, I think that, if no accounts of the expedition should arrive before the end of this year, it would be proper to send to their assistance.

Two such ships as the *Erebus* and *Terror* should be strengthened for the service, and, in my opinion, fitted out in exactly the same manner as they were for the Antarctic Seas; I do not know whether there are two ships suitable for the purpose, if not, two should be built, as they would always be useful for surveying purposes, if not eventually required for the contemplated service.

In the present year the Hudson's Bay Company should be required to send out instructions for a supply of provisions to be kept in readiness at the more northern stations, and direct such other arrangements to be made as might appear to them likely to facilitate Sir John Franklin and his people's homeward journey, should any calamity befall their ships, and render such a measure necessary, as they would assuredly endeavour to make their way to the Hudson's Bay settlements, if their ships should be so injured as to prevent their proceeding on their voyage, or so entangled in the ice as to preclude every hope of their escape in any part of the Polar Seas westward of the extreme point of Melville Island, as the shortest and safest route they could pursue.

I remain, &c.
(Signed)   JAMES C. ROSS.

Captain Sir Edward Parry, &c. &c. &c.

Reply from Colonel Sabine to the Extract of Sir John Ross's Letter.

Woolwich, March 5, 1847.

1st. I never heard Sir John Franklin express either wishes or expectations that deposits of provisions should be made at particular points for his relief.

2nd. In a letter which I received from Sir John Franklin from the Whalefish Islands, dated the 9th July, 1845, after noticing that, including what they had received from the transport, which had accompanied them so far, the *Erebus* and *Terror* had on board provisions, fuel, clothing, and stores for three years complete from that date (*i. e.*, to July, 1848), he adds as follow:—

" I hope my dear wife and daughter will not be over anxious if we should not return by the time they have fixed upon; and I must beg of you to give them the benefit of your advice and experience when that arrives, for you know well, that even after the second winter, without success in our object, we should wish to try some other channel, if the state of our provisions and the health of the crews justify it."

(Signed)   EDWARD SABINE.

Outline of a Plan submitted by Captain Sir James C. Ross.

Outline of a Plan of affording Relief to the Expedition under the command of Sir John Franklin by the way of Lancaster Sound, submitted for the consideration of the Lords Commissioners of the Admiralty.

As vessels destined to follow the track of the expedition must necessarily encounter the same difficulties, and be liable to the same pressure from the great body of ice they must pass through, in their way to Lancaster Sound, it is desirable that two ships, of not less than 500 tons, be purchased for this service, and fortified and equipped in every respect as were the *Erebus* and *Terror* for the Antarctic Seas.

Accurate plans have been preserved of the method adopted for strengthening those ships in the Dock Yard at Chatham, and I believe also in the office of the Surveyor of the Navy, and which, having been proved quite perfect, will materially facilitate the operation, whether the work is to be done in the Royal Dock Yard, or in a merchant's yard, under the supervision of an officer appointed for the purpose.

Each ship should, in addition, be supplied with a small vessel or·launch, of about 20 tons, which she could hoist in, to be fitted with a steam-engine and boiler of ten-horse power, for a pressure to be hereafter noticed.

The ships should be provided with everything proper for the health and comfort of their crews, and every provision made for wintering, as is usual in ships sent on discovery to those regions.

They should sail at the end of April next, and proceed to Lancaster Sound with as little delay as possible, carefully searching both the shores of that extensive inlet, and of Barrow's Strait, and then progress to the westward.

Should the period of the season at which they arrive in Barrow's Strait admit of it, Wellington Channel should next be examined, and the coast between Cape Clarence and Cape Walker explored, either in the ships or by boats, as may at the time appear most advisable. As this coast has been generally found encumbered with ice, it is not desirable that both ships should proceed so far along it as to hazard their getting beset there and shut up for the winter ; but in the event of finding a convenient harbour near Garnier Bay, or Cape Rennell, it would be a good position in which to secure one of the ships for the winter.

From this position, the coast line might be explored as far as it extends to the westward, by detached parties early in the spring, as well as the western coast of Boothia, a considerable distance to the southward ; and at a more advanced period of the season the whole distance to Cape Nicolai might be completed.

A second party might be sent to the south-west, as far as practicable, and a third to the north-west, or in any other direction deemed advisable at the time.

As soon as the formation of water along the coast between the land and main body of ice admitted, the small steam-launch should be despatched into Lancaster Sound, to communicate with the whale ships at the usual time of their arrival in those regions, by which means information of the safety or return of Sir John Franklin might be conveyed to the ships before their liberation from their winter quarters, as well as any farther instructions the Lords Commissioners might be pleased to send for their further guidance.

The easternmost vessel having been safely secured in Winter Harbour, the other ships should proceed alone to the westward, and endeavour to reach Winter Harbour in the Melville Island, or some convenient port in Banks' Land, in which to pass the winter.

From this point also parties should be despatched early in the spring before the heading up of the ice.

The first should be directed to trace the western coast of Banks' Land, and, proceeding to Cape Bathurst, or some other conspicuous point of the continent, previously agreed on with Sir John Richardson, reach the Hudson's Bay Company's settlements, or Peel River, in time to return with those people to their principal establishment, and thence to England.

The second party should explore the eastern shore of Banks' Land, and, making for Cape Krusenstern, communicate with Sir John Richardson's party on its descending the Coppermine River, and either assist him in completing the examination of Wollaston and Victoria Land, or return to England by any route he should direct.

These two parties would pass over that space in which most probably the ships have become involved (if at all), and would therefore, have the best chance of communicating with Sir John Franklin information of the measures that have been adopted for his relief, and of directing him to the best point to proceed, if he should consider it necessary to abandon his ships.

Other parties may be despatched, as might appear desirable to the Commander of the expedition, according to circumstances; but the steam-launches should certainly be employed to keep up the communication between the ships, to transmit such information for the guidance of each other as might be necessary for the safety and success of the undertaking.

(Signed)   JAS. C. ROSS, Capt., R. N.

Athenæum, Dec. 2, 1847.

Sir Edward Parry's reply to the Admiralty letter is long, but it is only necessary to give the part applicable to the extracts of my letters, and which is given as the result of his communication with Sir J. C. Ross and Colonel Sabine:—

Haslar Hospital, Feb. 23, 1847.

As to any communication which Sir John Franklin had with me before he left England, with regard to expectations and intentions that depôts should be formed at certain places for his relief, I have no recollection whatever of any such communication, while it could scarcely have escaped my memory had it ever occurred. And I venture to add, that had any idea of this kind seriously suggested itself to Sir John Franklin, he could not have failed to make it the subject of an official representation to the Admiralty, as the only correct or practicable channel through which he could expect to carry out an intention of this nature.

I have before remarked, that Sir John Franklin, knowing the hostility manifested towards me by the opposite party, was not likely to communicate any suggestion or opinion of mine to them; but the paragraph which Sir Edward has gratuitously " ventured" to add, carries on its face such absurdity as to require only this remark, that their Lordships could have nothing whatever to do with the establishment of notices and depôts by Sir John Franklin, and that, therefore, his application to the Admiralty was wholly unnecessary and uncalled for. But Sir Edward's object, in " venturing" such a futile insinuation, is too obvious to require further notice.

Sir Edward goes on to say, he agrees with their Lordships, that "the time was not yet arrived," while in another sentence he says "it has arrived," when due preparations should be made for instituting, if necessary, an active search " for the ships, conveying supplies to the crews, in case no information should be received respecting them during the present year." After deprecating that of going into the expense of fitting out an expedition on the scale hitherto adopted, Sir Edward recommends that whalers should be employed, and that the northern coast of America should be traversed, and,—as suggested by Sir John Barrow,—that a small vessel should be sent to Behring's Strait; for to the improbable supposition the whale party continue to cling, that Franklin will make his appearance!

Reply of Sir John Richardson (dated Haslar Hospital, 21st February, 1847) to the extracts of Sir John Ross's letters is as follows. After acknowledging the receipt of Sir Edward Parry's letter, inclosing extracts of mine, he goes on to make the following observations. " I had many conversations with Sir John Franklin up to the eve of his departure, respecting his future proceedings, and I also received a communication from him, written on the coast of Greenland, but never heard him express a wish or expectation of a depôt of provisions being stored for him on Melville Island, or elsewhere, and knowing him as I do intimately, I must express my belief, that he would have preferred such a request to Government alone." Here, indeed, is a wilful perversion of the extracts of my letters, which never contemplated that Government should establish depôts of provisions for Sir John Franklin at Melville Island, or elsewhere, which it is evident could not be done without vessels sent for the express purpose; nor is it likely that Sir John would mention any suggestion of mine to that gentleman, who was not a sailor, and could know nothing of the necessity of complying with my advice, which was simply to leave some of his *own stock* of provisions at certain places. He, of course, argues with the rest, that if the expedition is not heard of next autumn, or January, " proper steps must be pursued." Those steps were to send such ships as the *Erebus* and *Terror*, to sail in May, 1848, and then goes on to a long description of a land expedition, chalked out for himself, which I need scarcely add has, as I anticipated, proved abortive !

I may here remark before proceeding further in my narrative, that the anxiety of Sir J. C. Ross to stigmatize my counsel as *absurd*, inadvertently admits the truth of my communication with Sir John Franklin, on the subject of depôts. Sir John Franklin, according to Sir J. C. Ross, had mentioned to him my promise, but only characterized it as " absurd." This is no small concession from one of a party who had hitherto thought it expedient to tell the same story, entertain the same opinion, and almost agree in the very words which gave utterance to their sentiments. We get from these unwilling witnesses, most reluctantly, the admission of the truth of my statement. But what became of this admission? Did the Board of Admiralty make any inquiry about it? Did they ask the only person who could have enlightened them upon the subject? Certainly not. They played only the humiliating game of a "tin kettle tied to the dog's tail," and, unhappily for the cause of humanity, and the credit of the Admiralty, the dog which dragged them through the dirt was a cross-grained and sour-tempered cur, determined to snap at my heels and bark me into a becoming state of silence.

I have no doubt that when Sir John Franklin did mention my proposal, to have a depôt of provisions from his *own* stock, that Sir J. C. Ross would characterize it as an "*absurdity*," although at the same time he knew that his *own life was saved* by my having, on our last voyage, taken the same precaution. It is, therefore, deeply to be regretted, that Sir John Franklin did communicate to him my proposal, as it may by its rejection, through his unsound advice, have led to fatal consequences! He then goes on to recommend that, in 1848, ships exactly like the *Erebus* and *Terror* should be fitted out or built on purpose, although I have heard him repeatedly declare, during our last voyage, how much better small ships were than large ones; and it must certainly have been entirely in order to oppose my opinions, and to agree with the rest of the Committee in opposition to everything proposed or suggested by me.

Colonel Sabine's reply (dated Woolwich, 5 March, 1847) to the extracts of Sir John Ross's letter, is as follows:—

Colonel Sabine simply says, "I never heard Sir John Franklin express either wishes or expectations that depôts of provisions should be made at particular places for his relief." From this reply it is evident that, like the others, he had perverted or misunderstood the meaning of my suggestion, which I have already said was, that he should deposit out of his *own stock* a part at particular places for his relief, on which he might (as I did) fall back, and save the lives of his crew; as in the event of shipwreck, or the necessity of abandoning the ship, it was impossible the crew could carry the necessary quantity of provisions to sustain life during a winter. The rest of the Colonel's letter is quite beneath notice.

It must be observed that in all these Reports, none make the least allusion to the mildness of the preceding winter, 1846-7, which was of the utmost importance, and *to me* seemed actually an inducement to send the vessels of relief, especially as it is on record that a mild is always succeeded by a severe winter (which unfortunately took place in 1847-8); but this was never taken into consideration, and, in defiance of the certainty of an approaching unfavourable season, the expedition must be delayed, whatever may be the consequence! Had these Reports on the extracts of my letter been submitted to me at the time, I could have proved that these insinuations were totally unfounded, as will appear by a subsequent letter from me, written after the facts came to my knowledge, in which I justly complain that I have been unfairly treated.

It appeared by the papers moved for by Sir Robert Inglis, on the 13th of March, 1848, that my nephew, Sir J. C. Ross, on his return to his wife's friends, at Whiteglift Hall, wrote the following letter to the Secretary of the Admiralty, volunteering his services.

Whiteglift Hall, Goole, Nov. 8, 1847.
SIR,
I beg leave to request you will be pleased to inform the Lords Commissioners of the Admiralty, that I am willing and desirous to take the command of any expedition their Lordships may contemplate sending to the relief of the expedition under the command of Captain Sir John Franklin.

I have, &c.
J. C. Ross, Captain, R.N.

To H. G. Ward, Esq., Secretary.

To which it appears the following answer was returned.

Admiralty, Dec. 10, 1847.
SIR.
I have received and laid before my Lords Commissioners of the Admiralty your letter of the 8th ultimo, expressing your readiness and desire to command any expedition their Lordships may think proper to send for the relief of Sir John Franklin, and I am to inform you, that their Lordships have much satisfaction in availing themselves of your valuable services on this occasion, and it is the intention of the Board to appoint you to the command of an expedition to be shortly fitted out for Baffin's Bay.

(Signed)   W. A. B. HAMILTON, Secretary.

To Captain J. C. Ross, &c.

E

Being quite unaware that Sir J. C. Ross had made the application of the 8th of November, and still ignorant of one made by Lady Franklin, I reiterated my application for the command, and with my plan of four vessels, on the 13th of November: so that, before the answer to his letter (which is dated Admiralty, 10th December), the Earl of Auckland was in full possession of my application and plan; but I received at that time no answer, excepting a simple acknowledgment of the receipt of my letter.

Having no desire to prevent those who have differed with me on the subject of the probable route of the missing ships from enjoying their opinions, to which some cling even now with considerable tenacity, my object is to complain that I was excluded from all the meetings and committees, public and private, because it was surmised that my opinions were in opposition. No one excepting myself had volunteered before his departure to search for Sir John Franklin, and there can be no doubt that he fully expected I would perform so sacred a promise, especially as it was in return for the deep interest and the praiseworthy exertions he made for my rescue under similar circumstances; and I can imagine his feelings from time to time, when he would probably exclaim, " I depended on Ross, but alas! he has forgotten the sacred promise he made to me so often before my departure !" He little thought that I had entreated Government to allow me to risk my life for his sake—that when all entreaties had failed, I proceeded not only without pay or any remuneration, but to the sacrifice of my poor half-pay and pension, in a small vessel of 81 tons, for the accomplishment of his rescue, at the age of seventy-three years; and had the *parsimony of Government* not refused to supply me with a year's additional provisions, I would have passed a second winter in the Arctic regions on his account. At a time too when the Government ships were depositing provisions at various localities, he did not know that, in concert with the Danish Captain Platon, we had purchased a vessel for the purpose of continuing the search for his fate, which vessel having, in August, 1852, foundered on her passage from Riga, became the coffin of that talented young man and all his crew, leaving an amiable wife to lament his untimely loss.

It is beyond the object of this publication to notice the various opinions which were, both previously and subsequently, forced upon the notice of the Admiralty and other departments of Government, and which the lamentable Report of Dr. Rae has proved to be absurd and unworthy of further mention. But I am here in duty bound to declare that I was excluded in the committee which was instituted to inquire into the subject, and to report on the equipment of a new searching expedition; and it was with sorrow I found that, notwithstanding the loss of the *Fury* and the failure of the expedition of 1848-9, the members of that committee pertinaciously held to their former opinions, in favour of large ships as the best calculated for the attainment of the object in view. The only improvement was the addition of steam-tenders, although they also were too large. The command of this expedition was given to Captain Horatio Thomas Austin, who was first lieutenant of the *Fury* when wrecked in 1824, known as a zealous and persevering officer, and in every way highly qualified for the command. His second in command, and indeed all his officers proved themselves eligible and worthy of being employed on such an arduous service, and performed feats of travelling over the icy regions surpassing any previous instances. *Resolute* and *Assistance*, of 500 tons, with the *Pioneer* and *Intrepid* steam-tenders, sailed in May, 1850, but with the same disadvantage as the preceding expedition, of an unfavourable season for navigation; but with the assistance of the steam-tenders they were with difficulty able to reach the west end of Cornwallis Island, where they were all frozen in, as I had anticipated. The extraordinary proceedings, which reflect much credit on all those employed, have been published by the Admiralty and other persons, and need not here be dwelt upon. It will be seen that all the four vessels had narrow escapes, while the three small vessels were never in jeopardy.

When his Grace the Duke of Northumberland became First Lord of the Admiralty, I renewed my application, and I must acknowledge that it was most favourably received ; but unfortunately, Captain Austin's expedition had been fixed upon; the navy estimates had been settled, and his Grace, although favourable to my views, could not take upon himself the responsibility of equipping another expedition, and I was again doomed to disappointment.

Although I had not the honour of being consulted after the failure of the expedition of 1848-9, I took leave to submit my plans and to offer my services for the rescue of Sir John Franklin and his devoted companions, and I addressed to Sir Francis Baring, then First Lord of the Admiralty, the following letter, dated

267, Strand, London, 1st Sept., 1849.

DEAR SIR,

As the time has now arrived when news, good or bad, from the ships in search of Sir John Franklin, and as these ships in my humble opinion being of a greater draught of water than the field-ice, they are thereby more obnoxious to damage, especially as they would have to run more than usual risk, and the weather having been (by report of the Greenland whalers) exceedingly tempestuous, it is by no means improbable that the expected news may be disastrous. Taking these circumstances into consideration, I venture most respectfully to suggest, that a vessel should be prepared, and kept in readiness, to be dispatched with relief; and I am of opinion, that the 16th of September would not be too late for her to sail on that important service. I find that there is a vessel at Woolwich that would suit admirably. But she and my own little yacht (as a retreat vessel), which is also at Woolwich, should be towed round to Portsmouth, ready to be victualled, and would incur very little expense; and, even if not wanted, would show the public that your Lordships had not neglected any means which had the least chance of securing the unfortunate Franklin and his fellow-sufferers. I have recommended Portsmouth as the starting port, as being nearer and a better outlet than going round by Shetland. I need scarcely add, that I am a volunteer for this service, and I have no hesitation in pledging to reach Lancaster Sound, with the help of a steamer as far as Davis' Straits, if I sailed before the 17th of September. I shall not attempt to apologise for this trespass on your attention, and trust that your candour will excuse my zeal in the cause of humanity, even if you disapprove of the step I have taken.

I have the honour to be, &c.

JOHN ROSS, Captain, R.N.

To this I received no answer.

But on the 4th of January, 1850, I wrote to John Parker, Esq., who had then succeeded to be the Secretary to the Admiralty, the following letter, dated as above:—

SIR,

Herewith you will receive Enclosure No. 1, being the "Outline of a Plan for affording Relief to the Expedition under the command of Sir John Franklin, from the eastward or by the way of Baffin's Bay;" and No. 2, being a statement of my peculiar claims for the command of the vessels that may be employed on that service; and I have to request that you will be pleased to lay the same before my Lords Commissioners of the Admiralty.

I have the honour, &c.

JOHN ROSS, Captain, R.N.

Outline of a Plan for affording Relief to the Expedition under the command of Sir John Franklin, from the eastward or by the way of Baffin's Bay.

As vessels destined to navigate the Arctic Seas must necessarily be exposed to the collision of fields of ice, which are frequently set in motion by the winds, tides, and currents ; and as it is evident (as indeed most fully proved during my late voyage) that small vessels cannot only withstand more pressure than large ships, which have hitherto been employed, as they will rise to the pressure of the ice, but are less obnoxious to injury from drawing less water than the ice, which by grounding first on rocks, over which they are often inevitably carried, the bottom of the small vessel is safe, while the large one is wrecked, as in the case of the *Fury* in 1824. Again, any damage done to a small vessel is easily repaired, as by running at high water on the beach, inside of a large piece of ice (called an ice harbour), which is to be found everywhere, the tide (that there ebbs nine feet) would leave the vessel dry. That could not be the case with a large ship. It follows, therefore, that small vessels, carrying an equal quantity of provisions for the number of their crews, as large ships do for their number, must be the best to employ on this occasion, particularly as there is a large depôt of provisions and stores at Leopold Harbour; and the expedition for the relief of that under the command of Sir John Franklin should consist of three small vessels, drawing under nine feet.

1st. A small steam-vessel, such as the *Asp*, lately a Portpatrick packet, of 112 tons burden, and fifty-horse power. She should be strengthened, and rose upon five feet (as was my late vessel, the *Victory*), to enable her to carry a sufficient quantity of fuel, and to have the paddle-wheels made to trice up clear of the ice when necessary. She should have a crew of twenty-four men, including the captain, officers, engineers, stokers, &c.

2ndly. A small clipper brig, such as the *Isla*, of Aberdeen, of 119 tons burden (a description of which is annexed), with a crew of fourteen, including officers, so that the whole number employed on the expedition would be thirty-four. The price of the *Isla*, fortified and ready for use, is £1100.

3rdly. My own yacht, the *Mary*, of 12 tons, as a retreat vessel. She is strongly built of mahogany, but will require a little fortifying. She is the same vessel I navigated, in very bad weather, from Stockholm to London, in 1846, and is now in the Royal Dockyard at Woolwich. She would be towed out, as we did a vessel of the same size in May last expedition, and requires no crew.

These vessels, fitted and stored in the usual way, should leave England in May, make the passage to the ice under sail, and reserve the steam for the passages among the ice.

The expedition should first touch at Lively, in Greenland, and there procure two Danish interpreters, who speak the Danish and Esquimaux languages, and also some sledge-dogs; then call at Leopold's Harbour, and from thence proceed to the western cape of the Wellington Channel, where probably the first intelligence of Sir John Franklin may be found,* and subsequently, according to circumstances, proceed to visit the headlands between it and Melville Island.

If it is found necessary to proceed to Banks' Land, the retreat vessel *Mary* should be hauled up at Winter Harbour, and left with nine months' provisions, fuel, and ammunition, which would secure the ultimate safety both of our own crew and any that may be found alive of the missing expedition.

If no intelligence of Sir John Franklin's expedition is found at the different positions in Barrow's Straits, small parties, consisting of an officer and two men, must be detached in every direction likely to find the missing ships, on small sledges, constructed in the form of boats, of " gutta percha," which would be capable of overcoming every difficulty better than those hitherto used, as dogs can easily draw small sledges, but not large ones.

Lastly, it is necessary immediately to secure the services of the seamen who have been brought up in the whale fishery, twenty-five of whom have volunteered to serve under my command; and it is of the greatest importance they should be secured. They are now waiting at Peterhead for my answer.

I am decidedly of opinion, that with the plan I have suggested I could perform this important service during the summer and autumn months, and I have no hesitation in pledging my word that I shall return in October next, after having decided the fate of Sir John Franklin and his devoted companions.

I have, &c.

JOHN ROSS.

---

* At this place Franklin wintered in 1845-6.

Here follows the description of the brig *Isla*, new, 143 tons; value, fully equipped, £1100.

Mems.—Of the Claims of Sir John Ross for the Command of the Eastern Expedition of Relief.

1. As senior officer employed in the Arctic seas.

2. The only officer who actually promised to search for Sir John Franklin in the event of his not returning in 1847.

3. Having had communication with Sir John Franklin touching the positions in which he may be found.

4. Being acquainted with the Danish language, and by procuring a Dane at Greenland who speaks the Esquimaux language, he will be the most likely to gain intelligence of the missing ships.

5. Being perfectly acquainted with navigation by steam, which is indispensable (see his publication).

6. Has a constitution extremely well adapted to the climate.

7. Having been six years consul in Sweden, is well acquainted with sledging on snow and ice.

8. Doctor John Lee has promised to lend him the astronomical instruments he formerly lent to Colonel Chesney on the survey of the Euphrates, and also an excellent eight-foot telescope.

9. The men who have volunteered at Peterhead will serve under no other officer but Sir John Ross. They are all men who have served in the whale fishery.

(Signed)   JOHN ROSS, Captain, R.N.

Report of Rear-Admiral Sir F. Beaufort, K.C.B., Hydrographer of the Admiralty.

13th January, Sir Francis Beaufort to report.

Being thoroughly convinced that nothing but a steam-vessel will ever be able to advance through the Arctic Sea to any considerable distance, or retreat with certainty, the proposal of Sir John Ross to employ one of the Portpatrick steamers appears to be good, if she can be sufficiently fortified, and if the paddle-wheels can be made to elevate with instant facility. All his suggestions, indeed, are prudent, and the whole plan excellent, if he is really able and willing to carry it into execution.

F. B.

Copy of a Letter from the Secretary of the Admiralty to Sir John Ross.

Admiralty, Jan. 22, 1850.

SIR,—Having laid before my Lords Commissioners of the Admiralty your letter of the 14th instant, enclosing an outline of a plan of affording relief to the expedition under command of Sir John Franklin by way of Baffin's Bay, and a statement of your claims for the command of the vessels that may be employed on that important service, I am commanded by their Lordships to acquaint you that further search from the eastward has not yet been determined on.

My Lords, therefore, are not prepared to sanction any arrangements that you might have been desirous of entering upon with a view to the future; yet as they would be glad to be provided with those views in detail, in the event of a further expedition being equipped, their Lordships, without in any way binding themselves to employ you on such a service, would at the same time wish you to furnish them with a complete (proximate) estimate of the whole expense of such an expedition as the one you proposed to their Lordships.

I am, &c.
W. A. B. HAMILTON.

Copy of a Letter from Sir John Ross to Captain Hamilton, R.N.

267, Strand, London, Jan. 24, 1850.

SIR,

I have to acknowledge the receipt of your letter of the 22nd instant, by which I am informed that having laid mine of the 14th instant before their Lordships, you are commanded to acquaint me, that, though not yet prepared to sanction any arrangements with a view to the future, yet they would be glad to be provided with those views in detail, in the event of a further expedition being equipped; and that their Lordships, without in any way binding themselves to employ me on such a service, would at the same time, to furnish them with a complete (proximate) estimate of the whole expense of such an expedition as the one I have proposed to their Lordships; and according to their Lordships' desire, I have the honour to enclose the detailed statement of the whole expense of such an expedition, which I calculated as to the expenses of completing the three vessels I have named, ready for sea, from the opinions of several shipbuilders, and as to the stores and provisions, from the expenses of the *Victory*, discovery ship, in 1829; and as most of those articles are much reduced in price since that time, I have no doubt that my estimate will be found rather above than below the truth.

I beg leave to add, that I am confident that it is almost of vital importance to the success of an eastern expedition for the relief of that under Sir John Franklin, that the seamen brought up in the whale fishery (twenty-five of whom have volunteered at Peterhead) should be immediately secured, as the time has now arrived when they usually engage for the whaling voyage, and after they are gone, it will be impossible to obtain a crew so efficient.

In conclusion, I have to request you will be pleased to assure their Lordships, that I am perfectly able, as well as willing, to undertake this arduous service ; and I am confident that during next summer, if I am honoured with the command, I shall, under Providence, be completely successful in deciding the fate of the gallant Franklin and his devoted companions.

I have, &c.,

JOHN ROSS, Captain, R.N.

The estimates, which were enclosed, need not here be given in detail. The amount for the vessels was £3655. 12s. 6d.; provisions for two years, £1560.; in all £5215. 12s. 6d.

After the Committee of Investigation into the proceedings of Captain Austin and Penny's expeditions of 1850, in search of the missing ships, of which Admiral Bowles was chairman, had made their Report to the Admiralty, Government decided on sending out another expedition to search for Sir John Franklin and his devoted companions ; and the Lords of the Admiralty, after refusing to employ Mr. Penny again on that service, ordered what has been styled " THE ARCTIC COUNCIL," from which I was of course excluded, and which consisted of the following members :—Admiral Sir Francis Beaufort, Sir Edward Parry, Sir George Back, Sir James Clark Ross, Sir John Richardson, Captain Beechy, Captain Bird, Colonel Sabine, Captain Hamilton, and Mr. Barrow. No Report has been given to the public, but a splendid engraving of this celebrated " ARCTIC COUNCIL, DISCUSSING THE PLAN OF SEARCH FOR SIR JOHN FRANKLIN," was published by Mr. Graves, in which the venerable and talented hydrographer of the Admiralty is represented sitting at the table, with a pair of dividers in his hand, pointing out the position where the missing ships *ought to be* in the Wellington Channel, and according to the unanimous assent of the gallant *Council*, as unmistakably manifested by the countenances and the attitudes assigned to each ; while the portraits do infinite credit, as likenesses, to Mr. Pierce, the painter. But it was to a position where the unfortunate navigators *never were*, nor were there any just grounds for the supposition that they had ever sailed up the Wellington Channel. But it was known to the

Arctic Council, that Captain Austin and myself were decidedly against such a supposition, which was only supported by Mr. Penny to suit his selfish motives, which are sufficiently apparent by his proceeding to England instead of examining the west coast of Baffin's Bay, as he had promised to do, and on his arrival making an immediate application for another command; but whose evidence, and that of his officers and men, equally desirous of another lucrative *job,* had unfortunately influenced this celebrated *Arctic Council.*

The recommendation of the members of this *Arctic Council* to send large ships instead of small vessels, two of which, the *Lady Franklin* and *Sophia,* were actually ready for sea, while the large ships, being damaged, all wanted repair, can be considered only another instance of men pertinaciously adhering to an absurd opinion.

"Est stultum perseverare in errore ;"

for with such facts before their eyes as the loss of the *Fury* and the damage all the ships of Captain Austin's squadron received, it could be nothing else; as also the total disregard of the previous winter, which had never been taken by them into consideration, but by some called absurd.

I understand that the reason I was excluded from this so-called *Arctic Council,* was because they believed I was of a different opinion to them about the Wellington Channel, but which I submit was the very reason I should have been admitted; and having spent fourteen winters in the Arctic regions, it cannot be denied that I had some experience. Consequent on their Report, whatever it was, my plans and of course my services were declined, and four large ships were employed, which I foretold would be left in the ice!

Sir Edward Belcher's squadron sailed, May, 1852, in an open season, after a mild winter, and having reached further up the Wellington Channel than any other ships, were frozen in, and constrained by the succeeding severity of the year 1853-4 to remain there, a memorial of the folly of all concerned; while happily, the *Resolute* having reached Melville Island, the gallant M'Clure and his brave companions have been saved!

CAPTAIN PENNY.

After the return of the expedition commanded by Captain Sir James Clark Ross, in 1849, Lady Franklin, disappointed by the signal failure of that expedition, with that solicitude which has earned for her so large a share of public sympathy, repaired, without loss of time, to Scotland, to make inquiry among the masters of the whalers about her long lost husband; and among them she became acquainted with Captain Penny, master of the *Advice* whaler, whose surgeon, Mr. Goodsir, had a brother acting-assistant-surgeon of the *Erebus*. As this gentleman could not obtain an appointment in any of the searching ships belonging to the Royal Navy, he had, in natural and praiseworthy solicitude for his brother, embarked as surgeon of the *Advice*, in search of his missing relative. It probably occurred to this gentleman, who had still the laudable desire of continuing the search, that if a good story could be made out by Captain Penny, that her ladyship might have influence to get that ingenious and active navigator employed by Government, and that he might thereby once more find an opportunity of searching advantageously for his brother. Captain Penny having been twenty-eight voyages to Baffin's Bay (albeit he had never wintered there) pretended that he was much more competent to navigate those seas than the officers of the Royal Navy, and boldly asserted that, on the last voyage, when off the entrance of Jones' Sound, he had seen a cairn of stones near the entrance, and which could have been no other than one erected by Sir John Franklin. However, being engaged in the whale fishery, he had no time to examine it; but if sent out on purpose by Government, he would no doubt find not only the said cairn, but Franklin also. This plausible story had of course the desired effect on her Ladyship, who lost no time in using her own and her friends' influence with Lord John Russell, then Prime Minister, who, sympathizing with her Ladyship —whose requirements were so slight, asking only *two small vessels* to be purchased for Captain Penny to go on an auxiliary expedition to that already fitting out by Government—gave the order for the purchase; and a vessel building at Aberdeen, which I had previously advised Government to purchase, was bought at £100 more than she had been offered to me, and subsequently a second one, of less tonnage, was bought, and the two were in due time named the *Lady Franklin* and *Sophia*. As, however, the equipment of vessels was not the department of the Treasury, they were turned over to the Admiralty, and when the question of fitting them out came to be raised, Captain Penny very adroitly proposed that they should be equipped and stored at Aberdeen, in the same manner as whalers were fitted out, as he was unacquainted with the manner these things were done in the Royal Navy. This was acceded to by Sir Francis Baring, then First Lord of the Admiralty, probably from the idea that expense might, and at least trouble would, be saved.

The *Lady Franklin*, of 130 tons, and the *Sophia*, of 200 tons, were soon ready for sea, and Captain Penny, elevated to the position (excepting the rank) of a post captain in the Royal Navy, with double pay (£800 a year), with coadjutor Captain Stewart, as a commander with double pay (£600 a year), sailed on the 12th of April, 1850, although they well knew it was impossible they could make any progress for at least six weeks; but the early commencement of their pay was an important element in their arrangement not to be lost sight of.

The *Resolute, Assistance, Pioneer* and *Intrepid*, under the command of Captain Austin, having sailed early in May, soon overtook them, as also did the *Felix* and *Prince Albert*, having sailed nearly two months later, the former with the yacht *Mary* in tow. Captain Penny, having a command independent of Captain Austin, as will be seen by his instructions, destined to examine Jones' Sound, where he had boldly affirmed that he had seen Franklin's cairn. However, he had now heard that it was my opinion that Franklin had gone up Lancaster Sound, and of course, having no desire to let the reward of £10,000, offered by Government, slip through his fingers, we found him at the heels of Captain Ommanney, at the entrance of the Wellington Channel. He followed the *Felix* into the ice at Union Bay, Beechy Island, and never looked near Jones' Sound at all! At this spot I remained two days longer than the rest of the searching ships, and until the ice had so considerably broken up as to enable the *Felix* to proceed several miles higher up, and we discovered land at the bottom of the Channel, bearing north, which we named North Victoria, which notwithstanding he made a bet with me that land did not exist there, he subsequently claimed as his discovery! Having gone up to Cornwallis's Island, and convinced myself that Barrow's Strait was not navigable further westward, I was returning to take up my winter quarters at a harbour I had discovered on the west coast of Wellington Channel, when I unfortunately fell in with the *Lady Franklin*, and being informed that Captain Austin's squadron was returning to a bay discovered by the *Assistance*, and that he wished me to carry home his despatches, I followed him into the said anchorage, on the 13th September, and we were all three frozen in the next day. Time passed on; I found Penny an excellent and kind neighbour; he had luxuries which I could not afford, and was liberal in sharing them with me, while we assisted him in fitting out his sledges, &c.; and when the time arrived for travelling we mutually assisted each other. But I soon found that his ingenuity was little curbed by the unpropitious circumstances which surrounded him; he loved romance, and was detected in little exaggerations in his accounts in travelling in many instances—a discovery which was to us very amusing— he had named an island for his friend and countryman Captain Baillie Hamilton, the secretary; a bay for Sir F. Baring, the First Lord; and soon he had discovered water, and he would go in his boat to the Pole! But when he talked about his becoming M.P. for Aberdeen, Doctor Porteous and I began to fear that he was wandering, or labouring under a temporary aberration of intellect. At last it appeared that he had made up his mind to make a good job of the Wellington Channel, and although no traces whatever of Franklin had been found, after keeping his secret for some days, he produced two bits, one six, the other three inches long, which he said he found *upon* the ice, of American elm; at the same time, I saw one of his officers significantly put his tongue in his cheek, and no doubt they were purposely thrown *on* the ice for a piece of fun.

It was evident to me that these pieces of wood, being found *upon* the ice, could not have been thrown from Franklin's ships, because they would, in such case, like everything else, have been found *sunk* in the ice; but it

was not Captain Penny's game at that time to insist on
it being a positive fact that the missing ships had gone
up the Wellington Channel, because it would have
caused Captain Austin either to remain himself, or order
Ommanney to remain in the Wellington Channel, where
he used to say " I represent Lady Franklin." On the
contrary, when on the 12th of August, 1851, the question
was mooted on board the *Resolute*, he positively declared
that the Wellington Channel had been thoroughly
examined, and nothing more could be done, and no
traces could be found.   I had, however, at that time my
suspicions, and, addressing myself to Captain Austin, I
then said, " I am a witness to what has been said; but
black and white is better, and I advise you to write to
Captain Penny for an official report." This Captain Austin
did at twelve o'clock, and after much evasion, he received
it at four the next morning, of course to the same effect as
he had stated before me.   In a previous, and also in a subsequent conversation with Captain Penny, he agreed with
me, that the missing ships were wrecked, or that the crews
would be found on the west coast of Baffin's Bay, and he
agreed to search that coast, because he had an interpreter,
on which I took from him my despatches, saying it is 600
miles from Pond's Bay to Cumberland Strait, and it is
impossible you can finish that before the 1st of November.
I then agreed to search the east coast, and Captain
Ommanney and Captain Austin agreed to search Jones'
Sound (which Captain Penny had neglected), and Smith's
and Whale Sound.   Thus had Captain Penny so far succeeded in disposing of us all, and the moment he got out of
Lancaster Sound, he made all sail for England, to put into
execution his plan of a second expedition, with the addition
of a steamer—and of course not only contradicted all he
had said and written, but complained that Austin had
refused him a steamer, or he would have explored the
Wellington Channel and found the missing ships, which
he now insisted (with the exhibition and assistance of his
two bits of wood) that they had positively gone up the
Wellington Channel, and could be found only by a
steamer.   He arrived in London on the 13th September,
1851, at which time the First Lord and Senior Sea Lord
were on the continent, and his friend the secretary, Captain
Baillie Hamilton, could not undertake to fit him out until

their return; and in the meantime, the *Felix*, which had been unable either to penetrate to the east coast or obtain provisions at Disco for another winter, arrived at Scotland, on the 25th of September, and the whole plot was discovered, as will appear by the following correspondence.

Mr. Penny having been foiled in his hopes of obtaining another command for three years, at the rate of £800 a year, which it will appear hereafter to have been his grand and sole object, and the Arctic Committee having finally disposed of his services, he published a scurrilous letter, which he addressed to the Admiralty, complaining of the treatment he had received from their Lordships, and the Committee of Officers appointed to investigate his as well as the proceedings of other officers; and in this letter he had the imprudence to make the following reference to my name, by which I was forced to make a disclosure which could not but remove all doubt on the selfish object he had in view from the beginning.

Extract of a Letter to the Secretary of the Admiralty from Captain William Penny.

Adam Beck's story of the loss of the ships and the murder of the crews. The treatment of this by the Committee has, I believe, excited the surprise of every one who has read the Report. Surely, if they thought it worth while to notice such an absurd story (which Sir John Ross is the only man in the whole united squadron that believes) they were competent to express their contempt for it, instead of telling the Admiralty and the public that Sir John Ross attaches much weight to it, referring to his evidence where he states as much; they should have asked, if he gives much weight to it after the paper was exposed which he had witnessed and put his name to, and which the Committee refer to. It must be left to Sir John Ross to explain why the convicted liar, Adam Beck (who says himself, "Adam Beck no good, I lie!") should be believed in his old story, when made to swear it before a magistrate at Godhaven in Greenland. His subsequent deposition, the Committee says, was sent to Copenhagen for translation, and has not been returned. It is a pity their Lordships should not call for it and make it public here. I am indeed surprised the Committee should seriously suppose their Lordships capable of deferring another expedition in consequence of its not coming in time. I can only suppose it is out of compassion for another gallant brother officer.

Extract of a Letter from Sir John Ross.

It is with no less concern than reluctance that I feel myself under the necessity of noticing the vain, silly, supercilious attempt which Mr. Penny has made in justification of his extraordinary conduct, while in charge of a Government Expedition in search of the missing ships, in an ill-advised letter to the late Admiralty, which he has published. . . . Mr. Penny left England in the month of April, when (taking into consideration the severity of the previous winter) he must have been well aware that he could make no progress to the northward in Baffin's Bay, but his *double pay* of a *Post Captain* of the Royal Navy, to which he had been fortuitously elevated, became thus earlier payable; and he had an object in visiting Uppernavik—to procure from this northernmost of the Danish settlements the services of his *friend* Mr. Peterson, whom he induced to leave his situation of £20 a year,* without the permission of the Danish Governor, for the position of interpreter with him at £75 a year. In the month of August the *Felix* overtook the whole of the Government ships, when about the 12th of that month the aboriginal Esquimaux were seen on the margin of the land-ice, and had on the preceding day been communicated with by Mr. Penny, and whose note, delivered by them to the officers of the *Intrepid* and *Felix*, proved that no inquiries had been made by them respecting the fate of the missing ships. Adam Beck, the interpreter of the *Felix*, having obtained information from the *stranger* Esquimaux which he could not communicate (the *Felix* being then at a distance), Mr. Penny's interpreter was sent for, and flatly contradicted the statement of Adam Beck, calling him "a liar," which being ironically repeated by the poor fellow, who was frightened (and no wonder, as it is well known that these Danish overseers are often severe on the poor natives of Greenland.) In the meantime a young Esquimaux was brought on board the *Assistance*, and being tutored by Peterson, also denied the truth of Adam Beck's story; and every one as well as myself believed it was a fabrication, although no one could conjecture why he should in a moment have conjured up such a story, and *Peterson's motive* did not at that time become apparent. We all proceeded on our voyage, arrangements having been made that Mr. Penny, according to his instructions, was to visit and examine Jones's Sound (which indeed was the origin of his being employed), and the others to examine the positions in Barrow's Strait. But Mr. Penny did not wait near Jones's Sound for its opening, which could not be expected for

* I afterwards learned that, besides his house free he had only £5! and that he was sent back to the colony in disgrace, for being absent without leave.

some days, but proceeded up Lancaster Sound, where he spoke the *North Star*, and by her despatches were sent home; among others, a letter from Mr. Peterson to his wife, which will be noticed hereafter. We subsequently communicated with each other in Union Bay; and having remained in Wellington Channel two days longer than any other vessel in the · *Felix*, and owing to a disruption of a part of the edge of the barrier, we were enabled to see the land to the north of this barrier, which I named " North Victoria," but which was subsequently claimed by Mr. Penny as his discovery, and named " Albert Land." After passing Wellington Channel and ascertaining that the passage between Griffiths and Cornwallis Islands was closed by ice for the season, we were returning to Wellington Channel, with the intention of obtaining a position as far north in it as I could; when we unfortunately fell in with Mr. Penny, who informed us that Captain Austin's squadron were proceeding to a bay discovered in Cornwallis Island, to which we accompanied the *Lady Franklin* and *Sophia;* expecting that as nothing more could be done that season, I should be requested to return to England with despatches. On the following day we were finally frozen in, and Captain Austin's squadron did not reach our harbour.

During the whole winter Adam Beck continued to assert the truth of his statement respecting the fate of Sir John Franklin, and as he began to understand English, explanations and information were elicited from him, that convinced all on board the *Felix* that he spoke the truth. Before leaving our position at Cornwallis Island, I had several conversations with him in the Danish language, which he understands, and which convinced me that there was at least much probability in his report, and I demanded that a search in that locality should be made for the wreck of the missing ships.

It was, therefore, my determination to endeavour, even with the slender means and the small quantity of provisions I possessed, to make the search, which seemed to give much delight to Adam Beck, who exclaimed, " Now you see I *not* tell lie." I communicated to Mr. Penny that I intended to go round the north side of the main ice, and land Adam Beck at Disco, where I hoped to find provisions, directed to be landed there by the *North Star;* and he communicated to me, in presence of several persons, that he believed the missing ships had been wrecked on the *west coast* of Baffin's Bay, and, as he had an interpreter, he would examine the whole coast between Lancaster Sound and Cumberland Strait, a distance of 600 miles, and knowing he could not reach England before November, I sent no despatches by him. We proceeded to carry our intentions into execution, but found that the land ice from the latitude of 77° to 74° extended thirty miles from the

F

east coast, and as we were unprepared to winter, having only three months' provisions left, we had no alternative but to proceed to Godhaven in Disco Island, where we hoped to obtain a supply that would enable us to return to the northward. On approaching Disco, which we found quite clear of ice, we fell in with the Danish Government store-ship *Hvalfisken*, Captain Humble, who kindly piloted us into Godhaven. On our arrival I discharged Adam Beck, and, in conversation with Captain Humble, I obtained the following astounding information :—" I have just come from Uppernavik, and have seen Mr. Peterson's wife, who had received a letter from her husband, dated July, Lancaster Sound (which I read), saying that it was now certain that they would comfortably spend the winter in some snug harbour, and as he would be carried to England and spend another winter there, he would have plenty of money from the English Government, and that he would come out with Captain Penny, *who would have the command of another expedition,* and come home to Copenhagen, desiring her to sell his furniture, &c. Another came to his wife's sister, who is married to the mate of one of the Government ships—hoping that Peterson would be carried to England, as in that case he would return with sufficient money to enable him to quit this wretched country !" Thus it appears that Mr. Penny's plans, which it is evident he attempted to put in execution, by making the best of his way home, had been organized as early as the 23rd of July, 1850 ; but as he could not have left England, with the addition of a steamer, before the 1st of October, 1851, it was impossible he could have reached the Wellington Channel that season. His object must have been, therefore, to have comfortably wintered at Ball's River or Holsteinberg, or some port in Greenland, on full pay (£800 a-year), and proceed in June, 1852, and would have been just as far forward as though he had left England at that time. His plans, however, were happily frustrated by the absence of the First Lord of the Admiralty, and the decision of the Arctic Committee.

In the meantime Adam Beck voluntarily appeared before the Resident at Godhaven, and deposed as to the truth of his former statement, subsequently to which he was examined by Inspector-General Lewis Platon, who has written to me that he is fully convinced that Adam Beck has spoken the truth.

The following is the extract of a third letter I have received from Mr. Platon !

Montebello, Feb. 17, 1852.

From the interest I take in the question where Sir John Franklin ought to be sought, and being afraid, as you know, that Sir John Franklin was lost on his intended return, I feel bound to say a few words on this subject, which you will use as you think proper. I shall merely premise what you are already aware of, that I have for four years and a half held a responsible Government situation in Greenland. Three years of this time I resided at Holsteinberg, and had thus an ample opportunity of observing the character of the natives generally, and of Adam Beck individually, as he during that time never omitted an opportunity of thrusting himself into my notice, and he several times was temporarily attached to my household. I think, therefore, I may without presumption claim to be considered as not incompetent to judge of what confidence there ought to be placed in what may be deduced from such a document as his. From my knowledge of Adam Beck, I may safely assert that it is beyond a doubt that he has heard something about the two lost ships; but certainly it would be difficult to say what it is he has heard, merely by reading his deposition. As I informed you in a former letter, I have seen this man after his discharge at Godhaven. I therefore look on the deposition in a far different manner than others unacquainted with those facts undoubtedly would do; and I maintain that it throws a light on the fate of Sir John and his gallant crew, and that it would be shameful altogether to reject his evidence. I cannot but regret that you did not get a copy of the other deposition that he made, as it was far more satisfactory than the one you got. I must make haste for post, that leaves here at two o'clock, and must therefore conclude, angry with myself for not being able to write such as to convince any but myself that the greater reliance may be placed in his assertions. Pray write me as soon as possible.

(Signed)   L. PLATON.

Mr. Platon's letters, with my own, have been sent to the Admiralty. In one of them he says, "The people of Denmark think it strange that the English Government are sending to search for Franklin in every place but where he is to be found."

Mr. Penny must no longer assert that I am the only person who gives any credit to Adam Beck's assertion; but in return I must be permitted to say, that I yield not the smallest credit to the assertion of Mr. Penny, *that Sir John Franklin ever went up the Wellington Channel.* I was present at the interview he had with Captain Austin on board the *Resolute,* on the 11th of August, when I can testify that Mr. Penny made no application at that time for a steam-vessel; moreover I can testify that the application for a steam-vessel would have been absurd, as it was quite impossible she could have proceeded up that channel. The *Felix* was the last vessel that left that spot on the 13th of August, at which time the barrier of ice was still across it; on that day no water could be seen from Cape Spencer to the northward, and then Mr. Penny's vessels were both to the eastward of Cape Riley. Mr. Penny asserts that Captain Austin took the *Felix* in tow to take her home, that she might take the credit of his discoveries. But the truth is, that Captain Austin offered to tow Mr. Penny's vessels out of Lancaster Sound, which offer he did not accept, and it was then he offered to take us as far as Union Bay, Beechy Island, where Mr. Penny must have seen the *Felix* as he passed.

I have now only one more subject to disabuse. Mr. Penny's whole idea that Sir John Franklin went up the Wellington Channel, was from the fact of his having found UPON the ice two chips of wood, which, I verily believe, must have been thrown on the ice by some of his own crew, for otherwise they would have been found sunk considerably below the surface, and they were such pieces of wood as were numerous where the ships wintered. But if Mr. Penny really believed that the missing ships had gone up what he now calls the " Victoria Channel" (not marked as such in the chart he gave to me), why did he not remain himself to explore it in the spring? He ventured to say that he had not enough of provisions, because he had given some to the *Felix*, but this he denied on the Committee, as 2 cwt. of carrots and a bag of potatoes were all we got, and for which we would have supplied him with ten tons of coal and six casks of flour; but Captain Austin would certainly have supplied him up to three years; besides, the depôt at Leopold Island was within sixty miles of where his vessel would be. When I said in my evidence that Captains Austin and Penny were both justified in coming home, it was with the conviction that both thought and believed that the locality was completely searched, and that they both believed (as I do) that the missing ships never went up the Wellington Channel. I have no doubt that they lost both seasons, 1845 and 1846, and finding that they had only provisions for another year (and perhaps less, as many of Goldner's canisters were found with only *one cut* at the top, and being *convex*, were clear proofs of their putrescent condition). But upon this part of the subject I have some further remarks to offer; I shall, however, reserve them for a more convenient opportunity at the close of this narrative.

In conclusion, I deeply regret that Mr. Penny has been so imprudent as to publish what he had done; I believed that he really had been actuated by feelings of philanthropy—touching the rescue of my gallant friend Franklin and his brave companions. He had at one time gained my esteem and regard, and he knows that I acted as peacemaker between him and those whom his virulent temper had offended. I was an admirer of his zeal and unflinching perseverance, and I then believed that he had no sinister motive. It has therefore been with mixed feelings of sorrow and pity that I have been constrained to change my opinion of an individual, who has proved that he ought not to have been elevated to the position in which he was unfortunately placed.

JOHN ROSS, Rear-Admiral.

The above letter, which appeared in the *Nautical Standard* of the 6th March, 1852, was sent to the Admiralty, and duly acknowledged by the Secretary. I may mention here, that the Committee of Investigation was not only misled by Mr. Penny's evidence, but by that of Mr. Abernethy, in whom, from his insubordinate conduct and habits of intemperance, I had lost all confidence, and who on that day, being detached with Captain Phillips inland, had no opportunity of seeing the Wellington Channel; and yet (probably from a desire to serve his friend and countryman Mr. Penny) he said he saw (which he could not see) the Wellington Channel open; while John Jones, an active and trustworthy person, who was sent by me to Cape Spencer, where the best view of it could be seen, reported that the channel remained closed with unbroken ice! But Jones was not examined by the Committee. The *Felix* left Union Bay the next morning, and was to the eastward of the Wellington Channel before Mr. Abernethy was out of bed.

With regard to Captain Ommanney's evidence, it was no doubt conscientiously given, that he did not believe Adam Beck's assertion after what Peterson said, otherwise it would have been his duty to have remained to continue the search; but Peterson's motive had not come to light, and as it is now evident that the ships must have been lost on the passage home, I have no doubt but that, as Adam Beck asserted, one of the boats came on shore at or near Cape Dudley Digges, and which may yet be cleared up when additional traces are discovered by the proposed expedition, undertaken by the Honourable the Hudson's Bay Company.

I have now arrived at the point where my own expedition during the same period requires some explanation. In several conversations which I had with the late lamented Sir Henry Pelly, the Governor, and with Mr. Barclay, the talented Secretary of the Honourable the Hudson's Bay Company, my regret was expressed that those who had advised the Government had pertinaciously held their former opinions of large ships being the best adapted for employment in the search for the missing ships; and I said I should not be surprised if some of them suffered shipwreck, it being my opinion that some small vessel should be at hand to afford timely assistance. These honourable gentlemen being of the same opinion, I wrote a letter, through the Secretary, to the Honourable Board at Hudson's Bay House, proposing the purchase of a small vessel by subscription, under their auspices, and giving in an estimate of about £4000, including pay. In a few days I was sent for by the worthy Governor, and by him informed that my proposition was approved of, and that the Honourable Company had begun a subscription with the liberal sum of £500. I need scarcely say that I was delighted, as there was still a faint hope that I might at last be the means of the rescue of my valued friend and his brave companions. It was indeed only what I had anticipated, from the known liberality and humane sympathy of that Honourable Company; but it did not end there, for most of them, as may be seen by the list, added about £100 to the original subscription, including the Secretary, whose endeavours were indefatigable; till the amount of the subscription became sufficiently large to induce me, with the promise of £1000 from my munificent and worthy friend Sir Felix Booth, to prepare to fit out the expedition. 1 purchased a schooner of 91½ tons, at Ayr, from Messrs. Sloan and Gemmel, who were also liberal subscribers, and named her the *Felix*, after my worthy friend the baronet above-mentioned; and I appointed as second in command Commander C. Gerrans Phillips, an officer of tried courage, and furthermore possessing all the scientific acquirements necessary for such an enterprise. My old shipmate Abernethy was offered an appointment as master in one of the royal discovery ships, but preferred sailing in the *Felix*, as being, in his opinion, the most efficient for the service in the icy regions. Mr. David Porteous, the surgeon, a talented and highly educated young man, joined the vessel with the rest of the crew at Ayr; and together we numbered eighteen souls. The following circular was issued by the Secretary from Hudson's Bay House. I had provisions to eighteen months,

which were all my limited means couid afford, and finding
I could stow one year more, I applied for a year's provisions to the Admiralty, although, if not used, they would
either be landed at the depôt or paid for if not returned,
but was refused !

Sir John Ross's Expedition in search of Sir John Franklin.

The time for equipping Sir John Ross's expedition having
arrived, those who are disposed to assist the undertaking are
earnestly requested to give in their subscriptions without delay.

The amount required for the outfit of the expedition, including
provisions for two years, is only £3000—less than half the sum
subscribed at New York for an expedition having the same
humane object in view.

A groundless rumour that the expedition has been abandoned
has been circulated, which, there is reason to believe, has prevented many persons from subscribing.   It has also been reported
that this expedition is in opposition to that of the Government.
Nothing can be further from the truth, as the following extract of
a communication from the Lords Commissioners of the Admiralty
to Sir John Ross will show :—

Admiralty, March 16, 1850.

" I have it in command to express their Lordships' approbation
and good wishes relative to the expedition in question, and also
their authority to you to state the same.

(Signed)   " W. A. B. HAMILTON."

On the subject of Sir John Ross's qualifications, Admiral Sir
Francis Beaufort, Hydrographer to the Admiralty, thus reports to
the Lords Commissioners :—"With regard to Sir John Ross, he is
well acquainted with the management of steam : he possesses a
singularly hardy constitution ; he has acquired much dear-bought
experience in the ice ; is full of inventive resources ; and would
feel a degree of pride in carrying out this his favourite scheme."

The Hudson's Bay Company have set on foot this expedition
from a sense of duty—to satisfy, in some small measure, the
sacred claims of Sir John Franklin and his companions upon the
sympathy and assistance of their countrymen.   It is sanctioned
by the Admiralty, and is to be commanded by a Naval Officer of
dauntless courage and well-tried ability, who has calculated the
risks of the undertaking, and in humble reliance on the protection
of Providence is determined to carry it through, whatever it may
cost him.   Rather than it should be abandoned from want of
funds, he has devoted to its equipment the proceeds of his half-
pay and two pensions accruing during his absence, but it is con-

fidently hoped that the public will come forward with subscriptions sufficient to render unnecessary this pecuniary sacrifice in addition to his gratuitous personal services.

Let it be borne in mind that this is most probably the last effort that will be made to rescue from a miserable death one hundred and forty of the bravest and most devoted seamen that ever trod the deck of a ship.

Hudson's Bay House, April 4th, 1850.

Extract of a Letter from the Right Hon. the Earl of Hardwicke to Sir John Ross.

Sydney-Lodge, Southampton, April 9.

A man at your time of life undertaking on his own means so severe and arduous a service, is a rare and splendid example of devotion to friendship and science.

If my refusal to subscribe towards it would *stop you,* I would act on this selfish and stingy suggestion ; but as I see by the subscription list you are likely to gain the required sum, I shall give my mite to so good a cause.

You will therefore find £50 at your disposal at Messrs. Cocks and Co., 43, Charing-cross.

Wishing you from my heart all possible success,

Believe me,

My dear Ross,

Ever most sincerely yours,

HARDWICKE.

Sir J. Ross, 267, Strand.

This expedition was undertaken before that under Mr. Penny was agitated; and owing to the delay in obtaining subscriptions, and in launching and fitting out the vessel, we did not leave Loch Ryan until the 23rd of May, under the colours of the Northern Yacht Club, and registered at the Port of Stranraer. On the 20th of June we arrived at Holsteinberg, in Greenland, with my little yacht the *Mary*, of twelve tons, in tow, and having obtained as interpreter of the Danish language Adam Beck, we remained there until the 24th of June, on which day I entered my seventy-fourth year in perfect health. We were as many days at Whale-fish Islands, where we took in water and coals which had been deposited there for us by a whaler, and passing through the Waygutt Channel, we overtook Captain Austin's squadron, and was soon after that under the command of Mr. Penny, when arrangements were made and concluded for a simultaneous examination of every part in which it was thought probable the missing ships would be found, my opinion being (see my letter to the Admiralty) as before mentioned, that we should obtain the first intelligence of them at the eastern cape of the Wellington Channel; which turned out to be true, namely, Beechy Island, where they wintered.

The following extract of a letter to the Admiralty will best describe my proceedings until the date of my letter sent by the *North Star*.

Felix, Lancaster Sound, August 22, 1850.

On the 13th of August natives were discovered on the ice near Cape York, with whom it was deemed advisable to communicate. On this service Lieut. Cator, of the *Intrepid*, was detached on the part of Captain Austin, and on my part Commander Phillips, with our Esquimaux interpreter, in the whale boat of the *Felix*. It was found by Lieut. Cator, that Mr. Penny had left with the natives a note, but only relative to the state of the navigation; however, when Commander Phillips arrived, the Esquimaux, seeing one apparently of their own nation in the whale boat, came immediately to him, when a long conversation took place, the purport of which could not be made known, as the interpreter could not explain himself to any one either in the *Intrepid* or the whale boat (as he understands only the Danish besides his own language) until he was brought on board the *Prince Albert*, where John Smith, who had been some years at the Hudson's Bay settlement at Churchhill, and understands a little of the language, was able to give some explanation as to Adam Beck's information; which was deemed of such importance that Captains Ommanney, Phillips, and Forsyth proceeded in the *Intrepid* to the *Resolute*; and it was decided by Captain Austin to send for the Danish interpreter of the *Lady Franklin*, which having been unsuccessful in an attempt to get through the ice to the westward, was only a few miles distant. In the meantime it was known that, in addition to the first information, a ship, which could only be the *North Star*, wintered in Wolstenholme Sound, called by the natives Ominak, and had only left it a month ago. This proved to be true, but the interpretation of the Dane was totally at variance with the information given by the other, who, although for obvious reasons, he did not dare to contradict the Dane, subsequently maintained the truth of his statement; which induced Captain Austin to despatch the *Intrepid* with Captains Ommanney and Phillips, taking with them both our interpreters, Adam Beck, and a young native who had been persuaded to come as one of the crew of the *Assistance*, to examine Wolstenholme Sound. In the meantime it had been unanimously decided that no alteration should be made in our previous arrangement, it being obvious that while there remained a chance of saving the lives of those of the missing ships who may yet be alive, a further search for those who had perished should be postponed, and accordingly, the *Resolute, Pioneer*, and *Prince Albert* parted company on the 13th. It is here unnecessary to give reports made to me by Commander Phillips, which are, of course, transmitted by me to the Secretary of the Hudson's Bay Company, which, with the information written in the Esquimaux language by Adam Beck, will no doubt be sent to you for their Lordships' information ; and it will be manifest by these reports that Commander Phillips has performed his duty with sagacity, circumspection, and address, which do him infinite credit, although it is only such as I must have expected from so intelligent an officer. And I have much satisfaction in adding, that it has been mainly owing to his zeal and activity that I was able, under disadvantageous circumstances, to overtake her Majesty's ships ; while, by his scientific acquirements and accuracy in surveying, he has been able to make many important corrections and valuable additions to the charts of this much frequented eastern side of Baffin's Bay, which has been more closely observed and navigated by us than by any former expedition, and much to my satisfaction confirming the latitude and longitude of every headland I had an opportunity of laying down in the year 1818.

I have only to add, I have much satisfaction in co-operating with her Majesty's expedition. With such support, and with two such vessels, so particularly adapted for the service, no exertion shall be wanting on my part. I cannot conclude this letter without acknowledging my obligations to Captain Austin and Captain Ommanney for the assistance they afforded me, and for the cordiality and courtesy with which I have been treated by these distinguished officers, and others of the ships under their orders. Animated as we are with an ardent and sincere desire to rescue our imperilled countrymen, I confidently trust that our united exertions and humble endeavours may, under a merciful Providence, be completely successful.

I am, with truth and regard, &c.,

JOHN ROSS.

The sequel of this voyage has been published both in the Parliamentary Reports and by several who served in the expeditions, and need not be further alluded to, excepting as to the report of the small vessels, although exposed to great pressure. Mr. Penny, in his letter to the Admiralty, says, "I am sure their Lordships will be pleased to hear that my little vessels sustained an immense pressure in North-east Bay, on the 13th ult. (May), without the slightest damage, and that they have otherwise shown themselves all that I could wish."—(N.B. The *Lady Franklin* was the vessel I recommended Government to purchase.) The *Felix* on several occasions sustained very severe pressure, without the smallest damage.

The voyages made by that enterprising and talented officer, Lieutenant now Captain Inglefield, which obtained his well-merited promotion, are before the public, and require no comment excepting what is contained in the following letter to the Secretary of the Admiralty, which fully explains its object—and is in answer to an extract of that officer's report of his voyage in the *Prince Albert*, in the extraordinary open season of 1852, after a very mild winter. To which is added, an extract of my letter to the Secretary of the Admiralty touching Sir Edward Belcher's Expedition, and since which my anticipations have been so fully realised.

London, 22nd Nov., 1852.

Although we believe that Sir Edward Belcher's Expedition will not obtain any further information of the fate of the missing ships, those under the command of Captains Collinson and McClure may possibly require assistance, and therefore the expedition was highly necessary. But the main object of this letter is to call the attention of Government and the public to the most probable position of all the vessels now employed on that interesting service.

If Sir Edward Belcher or Captain Kellett succeed in finding a north-west passage, they will be heard of in the month of March next; but if not, they will most probably be *inextricably* frozen in, because on reference to the records of Greenland for thirty years, it appears that all open or mild seasons, such as the last, have been succeeded by several of great severity, as was the case with us in the *Victory;* consequently, according to their orders not to risk two winters, they will have to abandon their ships in the autumn of 1853, and proceed to the depôt ship *North Star;* and as it is even probable that she, having then 250 officers and men on board, may not be able to extricate herself, and taking also into consideration the possibility that the crews of the *Enterprise* and *Investigator* may likewise be on board—it will become highly necessary to despatch relief in the spring of 1854 at furthest. We regret to observe that all accounts from the north agree that the winter has set in with unusual severity.

JOHN ROSS, Rear-Admiral.

THE EXPEDITIONS NOW IN SEARCH OF THE MISSING SHIPS.

To Augustus Stafford, Esq., M.P., Secretary to the Admiralty.

SIR,

In reference to an official letter from Captain Inglefield, dated the 16th September, off Cape Adair, Baffin's Bay, to the Secretary of the Admiralty, in which I observe the name of "Adam Beck," who was interpreter with me in the *Felix*, has been mentioned in a manner that calls for some explanation from me, I beg, therefore, through you, most respectfully to disabuse their Lordships on that interesting matter by the following remarks :—

1st. By Captain Inglefield's own account he has passed the *only* place where Adam Beck stated that part of the crews of the missing ships had landed, and where materials could be found that would identify that they belonged to the said ships, without having made any search there or within many miles of the locality.

2nd. The locality re-examined near Omanak was not "the reputed scene of the murder of Franklin and his crew," nor did Adam Beck ever make such a statement, or ever mention to me that any cairn was constructed, or the bones of the crew concealed in them; and I was the only person on board who could speak to him in the Danish language, which he understood. These misrepresentations, therefore, existed only in the imagination of Mr. Abernethy.

3rd. I regret that Captain Inglefield did not avail himself of my personal offer and written desire to give him every assistance and information in my power, and I should have had much satisfaction in pointing out to him the exact spot to be examined, and to have given him letters to the residents in Greenland, that would have secured him a good interpreter, without which a communication with the Esquimaux was more likely to mislead than otherwise; but I was given to understand that the intention was the survey of the west coast of Baffin's Bay. My letter was not answered, and my attempts both at the Admiralty and on board his own vessel were unsuccessful, and it appeared that he preferred the information of Mr. Abernethy to any communication with me.

4th. The statement of Adam Beck may or may not be true; but I emphatically deny that the misguided expedition of the *Isabel*, as regards that question, has in the smallest degree shaken the testimony of Adam Beck, or that the question has been for ever set at rest. This expedition, in corroboration of the reports of Captains Austin, Ommanney, and Phillips, has—aided by the mildness of the season—decided beyond a doubt that the missing ships never passed through any of the northern sounds, and if ever their fate is to be decided, it will be by the strict examination of the east and west coast of Baffin's Bay, with an interpreter who understands the Danish and Esquimaux languages.

5th. It is also to be regretted that the energetic endeavours of that gallant officer, Captain Inglefield—who appears, in an eminent degree, to possess all those qualifications which are conducive to the success of such an arduous enterprise—should have been unfortunately misled, and that the *golden* opportunity of an unusually open season should have been lost—for it most probably will, as in my own case in 1829-30, and, according to the records of Greenland for thirty years, be succeeded by several severe seasons, which may render the navigation of Baffin's Bay difficult, if not impracticable.

6th. But it has been the practice with those whom the late Government have consulted, and even the relatives and friends of the gallant Franklin, to treat my plans, opinions, and suggestions, as in this case, with unmerited contempt. But the time fast approaches when the Government and the public will find that all my statements have been founded on truth; and then, Sir, who will envy the feelings of those who have, *some from self-interested motives*, pertinaciously adhered to the needlessly expensive plans, and heedlessly absurd opinions, which have been the occasion of such deplorable results ?

I am, with truth and regard, Sir,

Your very obedient servant,

JOHN ROSS, Rear-Admiral.

London, 30th Nov., 1852.

With regard to the numerous documents which have appeared touching the expedition under the command of Sir John Franklin, which are now " cast to the winds" by the melancholy report of Doctor Rae; those who are inclined to amuse themselves by reading the absurd and supercilious notions which have, during these eight years, appeared in print, have only to examine the Reports called for in the House of Commons, and the Proceedings of the Geographical Society, and they will find themselves highly gratified—while they will be astonished at the tenacity with which some maintain their opinions in defiance of common sense. But I am confident that had my plans been adopted, and had my endeavours to redeem my pledge not been frustrated, a very different result might have ensued. But I trust that I have made it appear to my readers that I have conscientiously used every exertion in my power to perform the sacred pro-

mise I made, under peculiar circumstances, to my valued
and ever-to-be-lamented friend and brother officer, the
gallant Sir John Franklin, who, I trust, is enjoying the
rich reward of piety and virtue in a better world!

Thus far I have confined my narrative to the series of
events in which I have been more or less concerned, and
I hope that in speaking of others I have neither exag-
gerated nor distorted what I have deemed it my duty to
reveal. No personal considerations have in any way influenced the course of conduct which I have thought
proper to adopt; and if my strictures may in some cases
appear severe, I wish it to be understood that it is not
severity at which I aim, and that truth alone is the object
and end of my endeavours. Hitherto I have confined
my observations to the fitness or unfitness of successive
expeditions, and I have deferred up to the present
moment offering any remarks upon the results which
have been actually obtained ; and, I shall, therefore, now
conclude the task imposed upon me, by suggesting a few
remarks, which seem called for by the conduct of the
parties concerned in the miserable series of failures which
have crowned labours, bestowed with much affected pomp
and pretension. Results which lay a fearful amount of
responsibility upon some, and upon others have set a
seal of incapacity and weakness which the country was
unprepared to see revealed. Be it remembered that I
impute motives to no man, but when the cap fits, let the
blockhead wear his ornament, if he can, without blushing
It may easily be conceived that the position in which I
have been placed under the circumstances detailed, in
soliciting employment, has not been fraught with agreeable accompaniments, nor was it one in which a man of
independent feelings, or generous spirit, could embark
without some self-sacrifice; and, in the eyes of some,
probably the loss of a certain amount of dignity. It is
always mortifying to be refused the means of doing one's
duty, and that mortification becomes the more aggravated
when the supercilious assumption of neglect or studious
rudeness are superadded. I repeat that I shall not attri-

bute motives to any of the actors in the farce which has become the antecedent to the terrible tragedy forming the prominent subject of these details. I have no doubt all persons engaged have acted up to the amount of their ability, and even to the best of their judgment. I do not say otherwise than that their motives have been of the purest kind, but still it is open to criticism, whether in some instances they have not been led astray by prejudice, or their judgment warped by considerations which ought not to have entered into such a transaction. For my own part, I believed, and am still convinced, that it was my duty, by virtue of the sacred engagement into which I had entered with Sir John Franklin before his departure, to adopt the course which I have detailed; and no cold indifference on the part of official dignitaries, nor the wise saws and modern instances of official myrmidons has ever succeeded in subduing my courage, or in damping the energies which have been sustained by a religious conviction of duty. The last words of my lamented friend were inscribed too deeply upon my memory to be effaced by such opposition, and his last farewell ejaculation, "ROSS, YOU ARE THE ONLY ONE WHO HAS VOLUNTEERED TO LOOK FOR ME ; GOD BLESS YOU !" arose to my mind as often as some fresh obstacle interfered between me and the obvious dictates of the obligation cast upon me.

I have already detailed the circumstances which led to the fitting-out of the expedition commanded by Sir James Clark Ross, together with an account of my fruitless efforts to procure such an expedition as I thought, under Divine Providence, seemed the best calculated to avert the threatened calamity, and which, it is now but too certain, we must deplore. It is unnecessary for me, in this place, to recapitulate my suggestions then made to the Government; suffice it to say, that I insisted upon the imperative importance of adopting ships of *a lighter* tonnage, not only because such ships were better adapted for navigation in the Arctic Seas, but because by means of the same amount of outlay which would fit out an expedition necessarily limited to a narrow range of search, several ships might have been employed *cotemporaneously*, so as to visit within the space of one summer the whole of the expanse of country which gave any promise of being the prison-house of the lost navigators. At this period, time ought to have been the essence of every endeavour, and by a well organized scheme of search, made cotemporaneously at different stations, skilfully arranged and completely co-ordinated, information might have been obtained and results secured, which, up to the present time have pertinaciously eluded the imperfectly-organized plans of search which have continued to succeed one another.

What were the fruits of Sir James Clark Ross's expedition? Absolutely nothing, although it is now perfectly clear that one of his travelling parties must have passed within a comparatively short distance of the very spot which Dr. Rae's informants point out as the scene of the frightful tragedy which his indefatigable exertions have revealed. If a greater number of ships, and a wider distribution of searching parties, had been at this time adopted, as I advised, it is more than probable that results of a very different kind might have been obtained. Nor is it the only misfortune that at this time the Admiralty listened to counsel which preponderated in favour of the course which was actually adopted; for, limited as were the means of search, as a consequence of the means adopted by selecting the *Enterprise* and *Investigator* instead of a number of smaller vessels, which might have been distributed over a larger surface, and have sent out well-organized searching parties, both to the north and south of Lancaster Sound, these disadvantages were aggravated by the mode in which the search was conducted, so as even further to limit its usefulness. Sir James Clark Ross, by an extraordinary amount of delay, which has hitherto been unaccounted-for, lost the chances offered by his first season; for he did not reach Lancaster Sound until three weeks after the whalers. And by this most untoward circumstance, any effective search was necessarily postponed until the April of the following year, when searching parties were sent out. And what could these parties have effected with the limited means at their disposal, and confined as they were to *one* centre of action in Leopold Harbour? Mr. Cheyne, with a party of ten men, was dispatched from this centre of action with *a week's provision*, and they swept over about fifteen miles to the westward. Another party got over about fifteen miles to the southward. Such puny efforts, compared with the necessities of the case, are too ridiculous to invite criticism, and, but for the stern and tragic associations of the expedition, one might be provoked to ridicule. In such a case, sober criticism would be out of place. Subsequently, however, a more serious effort was made on the part of Sir James Ross, on the 15th of May, when that officer, with Lieutenant MacClintock and twelve seamen, travelled to the westward from Cape Clarence as far as Cape Bunney, along the shore of North Somerset, crossing to the southward to a distance of about 140 miles, and then for lack of provisions returned to their ships. Here we are again met by the same difficulty which my plan of search would necessarily have prevented or obviated. It is true there were in all four different parties despatched from Leopold Harbour, but as they were necessarily restricted in their exertions for want of deposits at convenient distances upon a large extent of surface, the extent of their labours was exceedingly curtailed, and their result totally barren of any information or advantage. It is, indeed, exceedingly difficult to understand what was the real object of these searches. That they never promised any probable advantage must be too apparent, as their extent bore no comparison with the actual behests of the case, or the extent of country which ought to have been cotemporaneously examined. It is not for me to speculate upon Sir James Clark Ross's reasons for adopting this superficial and imperfect range of search. For aught I know, the same counsels which excluded my suggestions as absurd and unreasonable, might for a season have clouded his better judgment, and led him to adopt a course which I am sure under other circumstances would have done outrage to his judgment and capacity. It cannot be that he felt himself curbed and restrained by the instructions of the Board of Admiralty ; for, so far as is apparent by his own reports, these instructions were too little regarded; for it is in vain we seek to reconcile the actual course adopted by Sir James C. Ross with the instructions issued for his guidance by the Board of Admiralty.

In this manner were two precious years entirely lost. Sir James Ross travelled to the southward, to a point indicated by 72° 45′ north, and then retraced his steps to Leopold Harbour. It is now melancholy to contemplate this most deplorable beginning of a series of unsuccessful expeditions, which have cost the country the expenditure of a vast treasure, and uniformly led only to failure and disappointment.

It is not my vocation to enter into a critical examination of the conduct of Sir J. C. Ross on this occasion, nor even, if such a course were relevant, is it my inclination to do so. But I think that the failure of that officer is to be attributed rather to the original defects of organization than the faults which were undoubtedly committed by him. That the defective character of the expedition was rendered still more useless by subsequent events (to be recorded) is not to be denied; but in fairness to Sir J. C. Ross, we must refer the main cause of his ill success to the incapacity of the projectors and managers of the expedition. The great defect in the plan of the expedition was the limited number of ships, and their excessive amount of tonnage. If the same number of men had been dispatched in *four* vessels, the result might, and most probably would, have been attended with more success. By multiplying centres of action and distributing searching parties over a wider extent of the continent intended to be examined, the chances of falling in with the lost navigators would have been greatly multiplied, and it is now exceedingly probable that such parties might have fallen in with some of Sir John Franklin's people; for, according to Dr. Rae's statement, the advance of Sir J. C. Ross to the southward must have been nearly cotemporaneous with the passage of Sir John Franklin's party over the spot indicated by Dr. Rae. Sir James Ross left Leopold Harbour on the 15th May, 1849, and travelled to the southward, attaining his furthest point southward on the 5th June in the same year; so that it is highly probable that Sir John Franklin's party was close in the neighbourhood at this time, and must have been fallen in with had the searching parties of Sir James Clark Ross been skilfully distributed over the place of search.

There is one circumstance in this part of the case which must now be deeply regretted both by Sir James Ross and his coadjutor Captain Bird. Captain Sir James Ross, in his report says:—" We were accompanied for the first five days of our journey by Captain Bird, in command of a large fatigue party, which increased our number to forty-two. He (Captain Bird) would willingly have extended his valuable assistance still further, had I not felt that his presence at the ships would be more beneficial to the service, in sending forth such other parties and completing such further measures as I proposed should be adopted during my absence." Why, it may be asked, was Captain Bird brought away from a position in which his services were wanted, and kept for a period of five days, and then sent back without making the labour and time thus expended in any way available, as might have been done by distributing searching parties in this latitude ? If Captain Bird's services were required in Leopold Harbour, he ought not to have been brought away; and under any circumstances the labours of his party ought not to have been sacrificed to what appears to have been a most unlucky afterthought of Sir James Clark Ross. Why did not Sir James Clark Ross on this occasion, in obedience to his instructions, extend his search to the westward ? and why was this sacrifice of time and labour made without any apparent reason ? Upon the whole, I am sure that Sir James Clark Ross himself must be the first to regret the serious sacrifice of precious time and labour on the very threshold of the series of searches which have ended in nothing but a loss of treasure and an abandonment of ships. In looking at this first expedition, and without insisting upon the fatal error of employing *two large* ships rather than *several smaller* ones, it is impossible not to see that this expedition was, for want of plan and organization, necessarily doomed to failure. The effort of Sir James Ross ranged over a locality bearing an insignificant proportion to the whole continent to be searched, and as there was no reason why that particular locality should be searched in preference to the extent of surface which was entirely neglected, it is manifest that the chances of Sir James Clark Ross's success were only as unity against many thousands. The serious amount of time which was sacrificed before entering Lancaster Sound was also a most fatal mistake ; and this postponement of any serious effort, and absolute loss of opportunity, as we now know it to have been, was never afterwards compensated. I shall not take upon myself the invidious task of distinguishing any one individually as the author of this great and fatal blunder, nor shall I

seek to apportion responsibility between the Arctic Coun-
cillors and the Board of Admiralty ; but there were men
of experience who approved of this arrangement, and it is
difficult now to understand what could have been their
object, believing as I do—and all subsequent experience
has proved my views to be correct—that no navigators of
any Arctic experience ought to have believed, or respon-
sibly advised, that it was within the limits of probability
that with such ships the objects of the expedition could
be attainable ; and I cannot believe, even now, that
it was ever the intention of the persons who selected
those ships, to have attempted to navigate them *beyond*
Leopold Harbour.   It is hardly possible to suppose
that the Board of Admiralty would have made such
a selection without availing themselves of the judgment
and experience of Sir James Clark Ross ; and yet, it is
still more difficult to believe that this officer would himself
have made such a selection ; for no man knows better than
himself that such ships were utterly unfitted for navigating
to the westward.   Let any one cast his eye over a map of
the Arctic seas, and in particular those marked out by the
instructions given to Sir John Franklin ; and then ask
himself whether two such ships as the *Enterprise* and
Investigator, united throughout the voyage like the Siamese
twins, and finally laid-up in Leopold Harbour, could
contribute more than the smallest modicum of utility in a
search which required a distribution from six to twelve
parties at least, properly organized, with depôts of provisions, and distant and well co-ordinated centres of action
and relief in case of necessity ?   All that was done on this
occasion was a partial examination in Barrow's Strait and
to the westward of Leopold Harbour, to about 95° 53'
Long. W., and from thence along the western coast of
North Somerset, to about 72° 45' Lat. N.; and, be it
remembered, in a direction which offered no greater promise of success than other parts which were left entirely
unexamined.   If we had nothing more to complain of
than the mere sacrifice of treasure which this expedition
cost, it would be a matter of little consequence ; but when
it is recollected—as subsequent discoveries have shown—
that at least a portion, and an important one, of the party
of Sir John Franklin was wandering within 150 miles of
Sir James Clark Ross's party, on the brink of famine,

and probably worn-out by disease, calamity, and fatigue, it is impossible not to regard this parsimonious exercise of effort and fatal loss of time as one of the greatest calamities that has ever befallen our happy country. What extraordinary infatuation could have induced Sir James Ross in the first instance to have lost three weeks before entering Lancaster Sound? and what but the veriest passion for inactivity could have induced him to lay-up on the 11th September—a period of the year so far from being severe in these regions under ordinary circumstances, that it is said, by those competent to afford information upon the subject, that three out of every five days which elapsed between the 11th September and the 1st November, after the laying-up of the ships, would have furnished the means of getting the ships out of harbour, had such a course been deemed expedient. A witness, in all respects competent to offer testimony, stated that on the 11th September, the day on which the ships entered the harbour, Regent's Inlet was perfectly clear of ice, and the lowest degree of temperature recorded was, of the air, 27°, and of the sea, 30°. Even so late as the 19th of the same month, the mouth of the harbour was clear of ice, and on the 22nd the ice in the harbour was so loose and unconnected that it broke away from the land and drifted out to sea; and, indeed, it was not until the 28th that the ice assumed that degree of solidity which rendered it an obstacle in the way of the expedition, while at this late period Barrow's Strait still remained clear of ice. I ask, then, why this inaction from the 11th September until the 28th of the month, unless it was that the *Enterprise* and *Investigator* were utterly unfitted for the service in which they were engaged?

On the return of Sir James Clark Ross, the Board of Admiralty, by some extraordinary intellectual process, which has never yet been explained, suddenly adopted different views and opinions to those which they had entertained a year before. They now looked to Behring's Straits as the probable scene of Sir John Franklin's imprisonment. It would appear that the advisers of their Lordships, in May, 1848, entertained the opinion that Sir John Franklin might be found somewhere about Lancaster Sound, Barrow Strait, or elsewhere to the westward

of Cape Walker; but although Sir James Clark Ross
failed in bringing home any evidence which could either
confirm, modify, or contradict these views, the Board gratuitously determined to send out an expedition by way of
Behring's Straits. If such an expedition had been despatched upon an extensive plan of search, co-ordinating
the course through Lancaster Sound, and the extensive
portion of the earth between Baffin's Bay and Behring's
Straits, the boldness of the undertaking would have commanded our admiration; but being what it actually was, an
isolated expedition, it offered no promise of success, and
was in the last degree chimerical, if not absurd, having
regard to the then state of information on the subject. The
several expeditions which succeeded this were all open
to the objections which I have previously stated. There
was no sufficient distribution of searching parties—no
plan, nor organization, which would secure an adequate
examination. Ship after ship passed over the same
ground, and, in one instance, as many as six were con-
centrated in the Wellington Channel at the same time.
If ever plan and organization of parts were necessary in
any case, it was in a search having for its object the
recovery and relief of the lost navigators; and yet, strange
to say, from the first to the last, no plan of search
was ever preconcerted; and the consequence was, that
the examinations made were regulated entirely by the
accident of the mere locality where the ships happened to
winter. Of course, the results of such a system could not
be otherwise than a series of failures, and but for the
single-handed exertions of Dr. Rae, we might yet be
without a tittle of evidence upon the fate of the much-
lamented Sir John Franklin and the one hundred and
thirty-seven brave fellows who most probably shared with
him his melancholy fate.

It remains for me to offer a few remarks upon the
recent discoveries of Dr. Rae; and it affords me real gra-
tification to have found an opportunity of expressing my
warm admiration of his labours. It is impossible, however, to read Dr. Rae's Report without feeling that in some
important particulars it requires confirmation by evidence
of a very superior character to that upon which at present
it entirely rests. All that we really know, with any degree
of certainty, about Sir John Franklin, amounts to this,—

that on the 26th May, 1845, the *Erebus* and *Terror* sailed from the Thames, in company with the transport *Barretto Junior*—that on the 26th July, in lat. 74° 48′ N., long. 66° 13′ W., Sir John Franklin was seen by the *Prince of Wales* whaler, being at this time moored to an iceberg, and waiting for an opening in the great body of ice in Baffin's Bay, in order to make Lancaster Sound. Lieut. Griffiths, who commanded the *Barretto Junior*, says, "We left them with every species of provisions for three entire years, independently of five bullocks. They had also stores of every description for the same time." The next information which has reached us was through the united expeditions of 1850, which brought to light evidence which clearly and satisfactorily proved that Sir John Franklin passed the winter of 1845-46 at the entrance of Wellington Channel. The three graves, and various fragments of stores, proved to demonstration that a considerable period had been spent in this position, but amongst these fragments, those to which the greatest share of importance ought to be attached, were a number of tin canisters, still containing the putrescent remains of what was once called "Goldner's Preserves." The number* of these canisters was sufficiently considerable to lead to the belief that it is probable this might have been the turning point upon which Sir John Franklin's expedition had been regulated. It will be recollected that, after a most rigid and laborious search, no records were found of the actual movements nor the intentions of Sir John Franklin: a circumstance of great importance, and leading to an inference which, to my mind, is irresistible. It will not be forgotten, that in the instructions given to Sir John Franklin, there is found the following direction:

"19. For the purpose not only of ascertaining the set of currents in the Arctic seas, *but also of affording more frequent chances of hearing of your progress*, we desire that you do frequently, after you have passed the latitude of 65° north, and once every day when you shall be in an ascertained current, throw overboard a bottle or copper cylinder, closely sealed, and containing a paper, stating the date and position at which it is launched; and you will give similar orders to the commander of the *Terror*, to be executed in case of separation; and for this purpose we have

---

* There were about two hundred.

caused each ship to be supplied with papers, on which is printed, in several languages, a request, that whoever may find it should take measures for transmitting it to this Office."

Now, I think, it is in the last degree improbable, having regard to these instructions, that Sir John Franklin would have left this point of his progress with the intention of proceeding to the westward, without leaving some intimation of that intention, and the intended direction of his course. Whilst, on the other hand, I think it very probable, that if he left this station with the intention of *returning homeward* instead of *advancing*, that he might, and most probably would, have considered the deposit of such an indication useless and unnecessary. I am therefore induced to believe, that when Sir John Franklin quitted this spot, he did so with the intention of making his way home. Of course, the question arises, What were the probable circumstances which would induce such a course on the very threshold of the expedition? My answer to this question is, that his discovery of the condition of his preserved meats, to the extent indicated by the discovered canisters, would have justly alarmed him for the consequences which might have ensued if he continued his course outward; and leave it exceedingly uncertain, with such evidence before his eyes, to predicate of the extent of the mischief which might exist in this portion of his stores. He would therefore prudently, under such circumstances, have returned home in preference to incurring the risk which such a condition of things threatened in the event of his reaching a remoter point of the expedition, where he would be out of the reach of the means of rescue or relief. Up to this point there are data which furnish ample means for supplying conjecture, but subsequently there is a total absence of any evidence upon which reliance can be placed, until the discovery of Dr. Rae.

The substance of this discovery is, that while crossing Franklin Isthmus, in 1854, he received from the Esquimaux the following statement—namely, that in the spring of 1850, about forty white men were seen travelling south over ice, dragging a boat and sledge near the north shore of King William Land. That they reached the continent by the ice on the west side of that land; that they could not speak much Esquimaux, and that their ships were supposed to have been crushed by the ice. It was also stated that they were short of food, and looked thin, and that they bought a seal of the Esquimaux. It was further stated that they were going south, in the expectation of finding deer, and that they were in the possession of tents. Later during the same season, and before the ice broke up, on a low shore of the continent (Point Ogle), about a long day's journey north-west of a large river (Back River), some thirty corpses were seen lying about; some in tents, others under the boat, which was turned over, apparently for shelter. It was moreover stated that some graves were seen on an island (Montreal Island). It was also suggested that some perhaps survived till the end of May, and that they had shot wild-fowl, because fresh bones of geese were seen, and much ammunition was discovered below high-water mark, which had probably been left close to the beach before the thaw. Various articles were obtained from the Esquimaux, such as telescopes, guns, watches, compasses, silver spoons, and forks, with crests engraved, a walking-stick head, of silver, with the words Sir John Franklin, K.C.H., engraved on it. Sir John Franklin's Hanoverian order of knighthood, &c., were also found. Some of these articles were purchased and brought home by Dr. Rae. None of the Esquimaux who communicated this information to Dr. Rae had seen the white men, either alive or dead, nor the place where they are supposed to have perished. They had received their information, and the articles which Dr. Rae purchased, from natives living further to the west, the latter of whom had actually seen the party travelling on the ice. The data thus obtained sustain a conclusion that Sir John Franklin passed the winter of 1845-46 at Beechy Island, and that in 1850, about forty of the party were seen near the north shore of King William Land, and that later in the same season, some thirty corpses were seen on a low shore of the continent, probably Point Ogle, and that some graves were also seen on Montreal Island; and the articles secured by Dr. Rae prove incontrovertibly that some calamity must have happened to Sir John Franklin's party, and that a portion of his companions must have crossed in this direction. The great difficulty is to connect the evidence discovered at Beechy Island with that found at the spot indicated by the Esquimaux. Sir John Franklin might have travelled to the westward and been lost in his progress in that course; or, he might have met with a similar calamity somewhere in his passage through Baffin's Bay or Davis's Strait. It may then be asked, what circumstance distinguishes between these two possible cases, and what are the known conditions which make one of these events more probable than the other. I think the fact that no record was left by Sir John Franklin at Beechy Island, at his wintering place, is almost conclusive, that at the time he left this station he intended to steer homewards; for he would naturally reason that, under such circumstances, the leaving of a record of his departure in that direction was unnecessary and unrequired by a fair construction of the orders under which he was acting. On the other hand, if he had left Beechy Island with the intention of persevering in his course to the westward, according to his instructions, it is impossible to suppose that he would have neglected so manifest a duty, imposed upon him by his instructions, to leave some record of the course of his progress. Even if Sir John Franklin had not thus construed his orders, still prudential motives would have suggested such a course ; and it is, therefore, of all things, the most improbable that Sir John Franklin would not, in such a case, be actuated either by an impulse of duty or a suggestion of prudence. I therefore think, that Sir John Franklin took his departure from Beechy Island to the eastward; but I shall not attempt to distinguish amongst all the possible cases which might equally have led to a calamity which the testimony of the Esquimaux seems to sustain. I must confess that, with the evidence hitherto procured, I am unable to limit any of the numerous possible cases which may have led to the same result. But there is one remarkable circumstance, supported by most satisfactory evidence, which leads to the probability that these ships of Sir John Franklin were crushed in the ice, somewhere near the eastern side of Baffin's Bay or Davis's Straits, and that they were abandoned by the crews, who made towards the spot where they were found, with the intention of seeking food. The statement of Mr. Shore, laid before Parliament, on the motion of Sir R. H. Inglis, is to the effect that, about the beginning of March, 1852, he was in company with a merchant captain of the name of Story, who had made to him the following statement :—

" In reference to icebergs, I know a captain, at present in Shields harbour, who told me that when proceeding to North America, in the spring of 1851, the mate who had the morning watch reported an iceberg in sight, ahead of the ship. On a nearer approach, the ice under the water could be observed shelving out to a considerable distance at the lee side, this acting like a vane in keeping that part to leeward. On passing as close as prudence would allow, two three-masted vessels were observed close to the berg, but out of the water: they were regularly housed, with their top-sail yards and top-gallant masts down. No human beings could be seen."

The statement of Mr. Coward, the master of the brig *Renovation*, the person referred to, was as follows :

" When near the east edge of the bank, in lat. 45° 30' N., wind N.E., fresh breezes and clear weather, as much as I could carry fore-topmast studding sail, fell in with icebergs ; one of which was very large, with field-ice attached to it, in which were two three-masted ships, having their masts struck and yards down, and all made snug; to all appearance, they had passed the winter together on the ice. At about 5 o'clock in the morning, when within one mile of them, the mate called me to see the berg and ships. By the time I got up and dressed, and on deck, my ship was abreast of them. I took a spying-glass and carefully examined them, to see if any one was on board, but could see no one. At the time, I did not think of Sir John Franklin's missing ships ; anxiety to get ahead out of the danger whilst the weather was clear from fogs, and being too far passed before I could make up my mind, caused me not to reduce sail, and examine them more accurately. I am since of opinion they might possibly be the missing ships."

Such was the substance of the statement made by Mr. Coward, who was afterwards circumstantially examined. Other witnesses also corroborated Mr. Coward's statement, so that the apparition of the two ships may be considered as well authenticated as need be. Of course there is no evidence of identity, but the description of the ships so closely corresponds with the character of the two vessels under the command of Sir John Franklin, that it is impossible not to feel the weight and influence of the statement, and arrive at the conclusion that it is highly probable that these ships actually were the *Erebus* and *Terror*, and that they had been deserted by their crews as they were then seen.

With regard to the evidence furnished by Dr. Rae, it must not be forgotten, that, excepting the possession of the several articles—a fact too pregnant of itself with information not to carry its own weight—is only *secondary*. None of the Esquimaux had conversed with, or had seen the whites, nor had they ever been at the place where the bodies were found ; but they had their information from those who had been there, and who had seen the party when travelling. Such evidence can only be taken for what it is worth ; and when it is considered by how many possible accidents it may have miscarried between the original relators and the informants of Dr. Rae, little reliance can be placed upon its particulars, though, upon the whole, it may be substantially true.

It is somewhat remarkable that a spot clearly indicated as holding forth considerable prospect of success, and which late discoveries have shown to be so, was never searched. Captain Beechy placed considerable reliance upon the importance of examining Regent's Inlet, *about the Pelly Islands*, in a letter of the date of the 7th of February, 1850, and it is believed that he again expressed the same opinion in a memorandum submitted to the Board or Admiralty. Yet no organized plan which would have included a search in this direction was ever entertained by the Admiralty. Expedition after expedition has passed over the same course, and crowded together upon the same spot, but nothing like an intelligent organization seems ever to have been dreamt of. Nothing appears to me more certain, than that Sir John Franklin would have obeyed his instructions, if no untoward obstacles had prevented the course of his progress. He would, no doubt, after reaching the longitude of Cape Walker, try to make his way to the south-west ; but I have already stated that I believe his ships could never, under the circumstances known to exist in these latitudes, have succeeded in getting so far as this to the westward. Again, if he found that a probability existed of a large proportion of his provision being unsound whilst he was yet in the Wellington Channel, he would not have risked a further westward progress, but would most probably have steered homewards, leaving no record of his departure. Taking, therefore, all circumstances into consideration, we are forced to the conclusion that the preponderance of probability lies upon the supposition that the ships were lost somewhere in the Eastern Channel, on their passage homeward; and that the ships, being locked in the mass of ice, floated up and down Baffin's Bay and Davis's Strait for several seasons, until they were ultimately liberated in 1852, the crews having previously abandoned them, and made the spot indicated by the testimony of the Esquimaux.

If ever the dictates of humanity, and the natural sympathy of our kind, were sacrificed upon the altar of party prejudices and scientific *coteries*, it has been in this unhappy case. To suppose for a moment, that the successive Boards which have from time to time despatched the several searching expeditions, were actuated by any other motive than an honest desire to relieve Sir John Franklin and his companions in danger, would be absurd. But it is impossible to acquit them of grave errors : and it is also impossible to conceal the fact, that they have exhibited a want of sound judgment. In asking for the opinion of a number of experienced officers, they acted prudently, and would have removed from themselves a great weight of responsibility, if they had summoned to their councils *all* whose antecedent experience had made their counsel worth having. This they did not do, and narrowing this means of information, as they did, by confiding it to a party who were committed to a particular set of views, they lost the only advantage which a candid and unbiassed deliberation might have insured. It was known that I was desirous of despatching smaller ships, and thereby distributing searching parties over a wider extent of ground. Such a mode of action was of course open to the serious objection that it would abridge the patronage of the Board of Admiralty. This would be alone a serious objection in some eyes. And as the majority of the counsellors of the Board entertained similar views, it is quite manifest why such hostile and determined opposition met my pertinacious endeavours to realize my own particular views upon the subject. We can now only regret that patronage and personal considerations were not entirely overlooked, in a case which involved the lives of one hundred and thirty-eight human beings. Doubtless, all concerned in this unhappy affair, from the originators down to the last searching expedition, have lived to regret the share which each has contributed to every successive failure. And though it may be now too late to hope for any successful results from a change of proceedings, yet am I inclined to think that the country has not yet fulfilled all that is due to the missing navigators, and although the field of inquiry is now narrowed within the limits of a small compass, it is not to be entirely neglected, whilst it is possible that a single survivor may yet live to reveal the sad history of the fate of the Franklin Expedition.

APPENDIX.

(A.)

Copy of instructions addressed to Captain Sir John Franklin. K.C.H., Her Majesty's Ship Erebus, dated 5th May, 1845,—

By the Commissioners for executing the office of Lord High Admiral of the United Kingdom of Great Britain and Ireland.

1. HER Majesty's Government having deemed it expedient that a further attempt should be made for the accomplishment of a north-west passage by sea from the Atlantic to the Pacific Ocean, of which passage a small portion only remains to be completed, we have thought proper to appoint you to the command of the expedition to be fitted out for that service, consisting of Her Majesty's ships *Erebus* and *Terror;* and you are hereby required and directed, so soon as the said ships shall be in all respects ready for sea, to proceed forthwith in the *Erebus* under your command, taking with you Her Majesty's ship *Terror*, her Captain (Crozier) having been placed by us under your orders, taking also with you the *Baretto Junior* transport, which has been directed to be put at your disposal for the purpose of carrying out portions of your provisions, clothing, and other stores.

2. On putting to sea, you are to proceed, in the first place, by such a route as, from the wind and weather, you may deem to be the most suitable for despatch, to Davis' Strait, taking the transport with you to such a distance up that Strait as you may be able to proceed without impediment from ice, being careful not to risk that vessel by allowing her to be beset in the ice, or exposed to any violent contact with it; you will then avail yourself of the earliest opportunity of clearing the transport of the provisions and stores with which she is charged for the use of the expedition, and you are then to send her back to England, giving to the agent or master such directions for his guidance as may appear to you most proper, and reporting by that opportunity your proceedings to our Secretary, for our information.

3. You will then proceed in the execution of your orders into Baffin's Bay, and get as soon as possible to the western side of the Strait, provided it should appear to you that the ice chiefly prevails on the eastern side, or near the middle; the object being to enter Lancaster Sound with as little delay as possible; but as no specific directions can be given, owing to the position of the ice varying from year to year, you will, of course, be guided by your own observations as to the course most eligible to be taken, in order to ensure a speedy arrival in the Sound above mentioned.

4. As, however, we have thought fit to cause each ship to be fitted with a small steam-engine and propeller, to be used only in pushing the ships through channels between masses of ice, when the wind is adverse, or in a calm, we trust the difficulty usually found in such cases will be much obviated, but as the supply of fuel to be taken in the ships is necessarily small, you will use it only in cases of difficulty.

5. Lancaster Sound, and its continuation through Barrow's Strait, having been four times navigated without any impediment by Sir Edward Parry, and since frequently by whaling ships, will probably be found without any obstacles from ice or islands; and Sir Edward Parry having also proceeded from the latter in a straight course to Melville Island, and returned without experiencing any, or very little, difficulty, it is hoped that the remaining portion of the passage, about 900 miles, to Behring's Strait may also be found equally free from obstruction; and in proceeding to the westward, therefore, you will not stop to examine any openings either to the northward or southward in that Strait, but continue to push to the westward without loss of time, in the latitude of about $74\frac{1}{4}°$, till you have reached the longitude of that portion of land on which Cape Walker is situated, or about 98° west. From that point we desire that every effort be used to endeavour to penetrate to the southward and westward in a course as direct towards Behring's Strait as the position and extent of the ice, or the existence of land, at present unknown, may admit.

6. We direct you to this particular part of the Polar Sea as affording the best prospect of accomplishing the passage to the Pacific, in consequence of the unusual magnitude and apparently fixed state of the barrier of ice observed by the *Hecla* and *Griper*, in the year 1820, off Cape Dundas, the south-western extremity of Melville Island; and we, therefore, consider that loss of time would be incurred in renewing the attempt in that direction; but should your progress, in the direction before ordered, be arrested by ice of a permanent appearance, and that when passing the mouth of the Strait, between Devon and Cornwallis Islands, you had observed that it was open and clear of ice, we desire that you will duly consider, with reference to the time already con-

sumed, as well as to the symptoms of a late or early close of the season, whether that channel might not offer a more practicable outlet from the Archipelago, and a more ready access to the open sea, where there would be neither islands nor banks to arrest and fix the floating masses of ice; and if you should have advanced too far to the south-westward to render it expedient to adopt this new course before the end of the present season, and if, therefore, you should have determined to winter in that neighbourhood, it will be a matter for your mature deliberation whether in the ensuing season you would proceed by the above mentioned Strait, or whether you would persevere to the south-westward, according to the former directions.

7. You are well aware, having yourself been one of the intelligent travellers who have traversed the American shore of the Polar Sea, that the groups of islands that stretch from that shore to the northward to a distance not yet known, do not extend to the westward further than about the 120th degree of western longitude, and that beyond this, and to Behring's Strait, no land is visible from the American shore of the Polar Sea.

8. Should you be so fortunate as to accomplish a passage through Behring's Strait, you are then to proceed to the Sandwich Islands, to refit the ships and refresh the crews, and if, during your stay at such place, a safe opportunity should occur of sending one of your officers or despatches to England by Panama, you are to avail yourself of such opportunity to forward to us as full a detail of your proceedings and discoveries as the nature of the conveyance may admit of, and in the event of no such opportunity offering during your stay at the Sandwich Islands, you are on quitting them to proceed with the two ships under your command off Panama, there to land an officer with such despatches, directing him to make the best of his way to England with them, in such a manner as our Consul at Panama shall advise, after which you are to lose no time in returning to England by way of Cape Horn.

9. If at any period of your voyage the season shall be so far advanced as to make it unsafe to navigate the ships, and the health of your crews, the state of the ships, and all concurrent circumstances should combine to induce you to form the resolution of wintering in those regions, you are to use your best endeavours to discover a sheltered and safe harbour, where the ships may be placed in security for the winter, taking such measures for the health and comfort of the people committed to your charge as the materials with which you are provided for housing in the ships may enable you to do—and if you should find it expedient to resort to this measure, and you should meet with any inhabitants, either Esquimaux or Indians, near the place where you winter, you are to endeavour by every means in your

H

power to cultivate a friendship with them, by making them presents of such articles as you may be supplied with, and which may be useful or agreeable to them; you will, however, take care not to suffer yourself to be surprised by them, but use every precaution, and be constantly on your guard against any hostility: you will, by offering rewards, to be paid in such manner as you may think best, prevail on them to carry to any of the settlements of the Hudson's Bay Company, an account of your situation and proceedings, with an urgent request that it may be forwarded to England with the utmost possible despatch.

10. In an undertaking of this description, much must be always left to the discretion of the commanding officer, and as the objects of this Expedition have been fully explained to you, and you have already had much experience on service of this nature, we are convinced we cannot do better than leave it to your judgment, in the event of your not making a passage this season, either to winter on the coast, with the view of following up next season any hopes or expectations which your observations this year may lead you to entertain, or to return to England to report to us the result of such observations, always recollecting our anxiety for the health, comfort, and safety of yourself, your officers, and men; and you will duly weigh how far the advantage of starting next season from an advanced position may be counterbalanced by what may be suffered during the winter, and by the want of such refreshment and refitting as would be afforded by your return to England.

11. We deem it right to caution you against suffering the two vessels placed under your orders to separate, except in the event of accident or unavoidable necessity, and we desire you to keep up the most unreserved communications with the commander of the *Terror*, placing in him every proper confidence, and acquainting him with the general tenor of your orders, and with your views and intentions from time to time in the execution of them, that the service may have the full benefit of your united efforts in the prosecution of such a service; and that, in the event of unavoidable separation, or of any accident to yourself, Captain Crozier may have the advantage of knowing, up to the latest practicable period, all your ideas and intentions relative to a satisfactory completion of this interesting undertaking.

12. We also recommend, that as frequent an exchange take place as conveniently may be of the observations made in the two ships; that any scientific discovery made by the one, be as quickly as possible communicated for the advantage and guidance of the other, in making their future observations, and to increase the probability of the observations of both being preserved.

13. We have caused a great variety of valuable instruments to

be put on board the ships under your orders, of which you will be furnished with a list, and for the return of which you will be held responsible ; among these, are instruments of the latest improvements for making a series of observations on terrestrial magnetism, which are at this time peculiarly desirable, and strongly recommended by the President and Council of the Royal Society, that the important advantage be derived from observations taken in the North Polar Sea, in co-operation with the observers who are at present carrying on an uniform system at the magnetic observatories established by England in her distant territories, and, through her influence, in other parts of the world ; and the more desirable is this co-operation in the present year, when these splendid establishments, which do so much honour to the nations who have cheerfully erected them at a great expense, are to cease. The only magnetical observations that have been obtained very partially in the Arctic Regions, are now a quarter of a century old, and it is known that the phenomena are subject to considerable secular changes. It is also stated by Colonel Sabine, that the instruments and methods of observation have been so greatly improved, that the earlier observations are not to be named in point of precision with those which would now be made ; and he concludes by observing, that the passage through the Polar Sea would afford the most important service that now remains to be performed towards the completion of the magnetic survey of the globe.

14. Impressed with the importance of this subject, we have deemed it proper to request Lieut.-Colonel Sabine to allow Commander Fitzjames to profit by his valuable instructions, and we direct you, therefore, to place this important branch of science under the immediate charge of Commander Fitzjames ; and as several other officers have also received similar instruction at Woolwich, you will therefore cause observations to be made daily on board each of the ships whilst at sea (and when not prevented by weather, and other circumstances) on the magnetic variation, dip, and intensity, noting at the time the temperature of the air, and of the sea at the surface, and at different depths ; and you will be careful that in harbour and on other favourable occasions those observations shall be attended to, by means of which the influence of the ship's iron on the result obtained at sea may be computed and allowed for.

15. In the possible event of the ships being detained during a winter in the high latitudes, the expedition has been supplied with a portable observatory, and with instruments similar to those which are employed in the fixed magnetical and meteorological observatories instituted by her Majesty's Government in several of the British colonies.

16. It is our desire that, in case of such detention, observations

should be made with these instruments, according to the system adopted in the aforesaid observatories, and detailed directions will be supplied for this purpose, which, with the instruction received at Woolwich, will be found, as we confidently anticipate, to afford full and sufficient guidance for such observations, which will derive from their locality peculiar interest, and a high theoretical value.

17. We have also directed instruments to be specially provided for observations on atmospherical refraction at very low altitudes, in case of the expedition being detained during a winter in the high latitudes ; on this subject also particular directions will be supplied, and you will add any other meteorological observations that may occur to you of general utility ; you will also take occasions to try the depth of the sea and nature of the bottom, the rise, direction, and strength of the tides, and the set and velocity of currents.

18. And you are to understand that although the effecting a passage from the Atlantic to the Pacific is the main object of this expedition, yet, that the ascertaining the true geographical position of the different points of land near which you may pass, so far as can be effected without detention of the ships in their progress westward, as well as such other observations as you may have opportunities of making in natural history, geography, &c., in parts of the globe either wholly unknown or little visited, must prove most valuable and interesting to the science of our country ; and we therefore desire you to give your unremitting attention, and to call that of all the officers under your command, to these points, as being objects of high interest and importance.

19. For the purpose, not only of ascertaining the set of the currents in the Arctic Seas, but also of affording more frequent chances of hearing of your progress, we desire that you do frequently, after you have passed the latitude of 65° north, and once every day when you shall be in an ascertained current, throw overboard a bottle or copper cylinder closely sealed, and containing a paper stating the date and position at which it is launched, and you will give similar orders to the commander of the *Terror*, to be executed in case of separation ; and for this purpose, we have caused each ship to be supplied with papers, on which is printed, in several languages, a request that whoever may find it should take measures for transmitting it to this office.

20. You are to make use of every means in your power to collect and preserve specimens of the animal, mineral, and vegetable kingdoms, should circumstances place such within your reach without causing your detention, and of the larger animals you are to cause accurate drawings to be made, to accompany and elucidate the descriptions of them. In this, as well as in every other part

of your scientific duty, we trust that you will receive material assistance from the officers under your command, several of whom are represented to us as well qualified in these respects.

21. In the event of any irreparable accident happening to either of the two ships, you are to cause the officers and crew of the disabled ship to be removed into the other, and with her singly to proceed in prosecution of the voyage, or return to England, according as circumstances shall appear to require, understanding that the officers and crews of both ships are hereby authorized and required to continue to perform the duties according to their respective ranks and stations on board either ship to which they may be so removed, in the event of an occurrence of this nature. Should, unfortunately, your own ship be the one disabled, you are in that case to take command of the *Terror*, and in the event of any fatal accident happening to yourself, Captain Crozier is hereby authorized to take the command of the *Erebus*, placing the officer of the expedition who may then be next in seniority to him in command of the *Terror*. Also, in the event of your own inability, by sickness or otherwise, at any period of this service, to continue to carry these instructions into execution, you are to transfer them to the officer the next in command to you employed on the expedition, who is hereby required to execute them in the best manner he can for the attainment of the several objects herein set forth.

22. You are, while executing the service pointed out in these instructions, to take every opportunity that may offer of acquainting our secretary, for our information, with your progress, and on your arrival in England you are immediately to repair to this office, in order to lay before us a full account of your proceedings in the whole course of your voyage, taking care before you leave the ship to demand from the officers, petty officers, and all other persons on board, the logs and journals they may have kept, together with any drawings or charts they may have made, which are all to be sealed up, and you will issue similar directions to Captain Crozier and his officers. The said logs, journals, or other documents to be thereafter disposed of as we may think proper to determine.

23. In the event of England becoming involved in hostilities with any other power during your absence, you are nevertheless clearly to understand that you are not on any account to commit any hostile act whatsoever, the expedition under your orders being only intended for the purpose of discovery and science, and it being the practice of all civilized nations to consider vessels so employed as excluded from the operations of war; and, confiding in this feeling, we should trust that you would receive every

assistance from the ships or subjects of any foreign power which
you may fall in with; but special application to that effect has
been made to the respective governments.

Given under our hands, this 5th day of May, 1845.

(Signed) HADDINGTON.
G. COCKBURN.
W. H. GAGE.

Sir John Franklin, K.C.H.
Captain of H.M.S. *Erebus* at Woolwich.

By command of their Lordships.
(Signed) W. A. B. HAMILTON.

(B.)

*To the Most Noble the Marquess of Northampton, K.G., President
of the Royal Society, &c. &c.*

16, Park Street, Grosvenor Square, London,
11th February, 1847.

MY LORD MARQUESS,

I have the honour to inform your Lordship, that during
the last spring, I had projected a plan for the double purpose of
measuring an arc of the meridian of Spitzbergen,and making another
attempt to reach the North Pole, which was to have been undertaken
by myself, at the expense of my patriotic friend Sir Felix Booth,
but which was subsequently abandoned by him, in consequence of
animadversions contained in the late publication of Sir John
Barrow, who, he said, might impute sinister motives. In May
last, I addressed a letter to the talented hydrographer of the
Admiralty, at the desire of the Earl of Haddington, the extract
of which I now enclose, will fully explain my plan, but which, for
obvious reasons, was never acted upon.

I have now been induced to renew my application to the Lords
Commissioners of the Admiralty. First, from the fact of my
having promised to Sir John Franklin that I would volunteer to
rescue him and his brave companions, if not heard of in the
spring of 1847, and nothing having been heard of the expedition
by the whalers that have all arrived from Baffin's Bay, the probability is, that the ships are both frozen up, or that some misfortune has befallen them.

My proposal is, therefore, that an expedition should be prepared, such as described in the extract of my letter to Admiral
Beaufort; and that, if no accounts are received from Sir John

Franklin before the 1st of July, 1847, the expedition shall proceed to Lancaster Sound, in search of the gallant officers and men employed in ascertaining the existence, or otherwise, of a north-west passage. But if, on the contrary, they return by that time, or if they have happily passed Behring's Strait, then the expedition under my command will proceed to Spitzbergen, in order to perform the service I have described. Having pointed out how the expedition could be fitted out at a very moderate expense, I have earnestly stated the necessity of commencing without delay the fitting out of this expedition, because it will be absolutely necessary to provide Lapland clothing for the officers and men, who are employed either in travelling from the ship to search for Sir John Franklin and his crew, or in travelling to the Pole, and this clothing can only be procured during the winter, through the Consul-General at Christiana in Norway.

Secondly, steam-machinery for the vessel I have selected, and the fitting out of both, will require a considerable time to be completed.

It having been intimated to me by Sir Charles Adam, the Senior Sea Lord of the Admiralty, that an application should come from the Royal Society, at whose instance the Franklin Expedition was undertaken, to the Board of Admiralty, I trust that your Lordship's candour will excuse my zeal for the advancement of science and geographical knowledge, and do justice to the sincerity of my desire to rescue the gallant officers and crews who are now probably looking forward to the promise I made to tender them assistance. And I venture to request that your Lordship, as the President of the Royal Society, will submit my proposal to the Council, and by taking it into favourable consideration, transmit to me your high recommendation and approval, for the information of the Lords Commissioners of the Admiralty. And I have now only to add, and to express my unqualified readiness to receive any communication made to me by the Royal Society, and pay every attention to their wishes that lies in my power.

I have the honour to be, with the highest respect,

My Lord,

Your Lordship's most obedient and humble servant,

JOHN ROSS, Captain Royal Navy.

The Most Noble the Marquess of Northampton,
&c. &c. &c.

(C.)

No. 6.

Sir,

I am to acknowledge the receipt of your letter, dated the 6th instant, and the therein enclosed copy of the translation of a letter written by Adam Beck, the Esquimaux interpreter of the *Felix*, being the deposition sworn to by him in my presence at Godhavn, in the island of Disco, Greenland, and requiring my consideration, and my report on the same as relative to the missing expedition under Sir John Franklin.

And I have to acquaint you, for the information of the Lords Commissioners of the Admiralty, that I have carefully considered the said translation made by Professor Nösted, and am decidedly of opinion that it confirms the statement often made to myself by Adam Beck, during the voyage, when I put questions to him in the Danish language on the subject, namely, that the two missing ships were lost on the east coast of Baffin's Bay in the Autumn of 1846. Had his deposition been more coherent, I should not have placed so much reliance on it as I now do ; because then it would not have been his own composition. Referring also to Mr. Platon's letters, before transmitted to you for the information of their Lordships, it will be seen that Adam Beck had subsequently made a more satisfactory deposition, and had been strictly questioned by that gentleman, who then held a responsible situation under the Danish Government at Greenland, and who is decidedly of opinion that Adam Beck has spoken and sworn to the truth, and the evidence he has given touching the fate of the missing ships ought not to be rejected in consequence of its incoherency and its contradiction by the Dane, Petersen, who did so for obvious reasons.

Having seen in the weekly paper, *Nautical Standard*, that Mr. Penny had published his letter to the Admiralty, in which I am called on to explain " Why I believed Adam Beck's assertion ?" I obtained his pamphlet, and in the same paper I have published the enclosed reply, to which I beg to refer, and which will account in a satisfactory manner for the disbelief (in the first instance) of Adam Beck's story, and the observations made by the Arctic Committee, and evidence touching the document written on board the *Assistance*, which arose from his being taken there against his will, to write down what the Esquimaux boy said (who had been tutored by Petersen to say nothing about the lost ships), but not what he himself had heard, and of course (from Petersen's contradiction)

Captains Austin and Ommaney believed that Adam Beck had been telling a falsehood, because otherwise it would have been their duty to have made a search in that locality.

It will be impossible that the expedition now fitting out can examine the east coast of Baffin's Bay, and the Wellington Channel also, during this season, besides which a knowledge of the Danish language is a qualification absolutely necessary, as the Esquimaux of Danish Greenland understand only the Danish and their own language; and in fact, I was the only person in the seven ships who could obtain the information from Adam Beck touching the fate of the ships.

And referring to my plan for effectually examining the said locality, as the only chance of setting the question at rest,

I have, &c.

(Signed)   John Ross, Rear-Admiral.

Captain W. A. B. Hamilton, R.N.
    Secretary of the Admiralty, &c. &c. &c.

Enclosure to No. 6.

To the Editor of the Nautical Standard.

Sir,

It is with no less concern than reluctance that I feel myself under the necessity of noticing the vain, silly, and supercilious attempt which Captain Penny has made in justification of his extraordinary conduct while in charge of a Government Expedition in search of the missing ships, by an ill-advised letter to the late Admiralty, which he has published. For being employed on the same interesting service, and our vessels being frozen up within two hundred yards of each other, and rendering each other every assistance in our power for eleven months, I have to acknowledge many marks of his kindness, in bountifully sharing with us some of those luxuries supplied to him by Government, which my limited means did not enable me to procure; a circumstance which was, without doubt, conducive to the comfort, if not to the health, we enjoyed during the severity of an Arctic winter.

I shall not, however, notice the many misrepresentations with which his almost unintelligible statements are replete, leaving Captain Austin either to refute them, or to treat them with their merited contempt. But I am called upon by Captain Penny to explain why I continue to believe the assertion of Adam Beck, and in doing so, I have to regret that I must make an exposure which cannot be agreeable to him, and which, but for his temerity in demanding it, would have been buried in oblivion. As, however, this circumstance is closely connected with the fate of the gallant Franklin, all personal considerations must give way to truth and justice.

Captain Penny left England early in the month of April, when (taking into consideration the severity of the previous winter) he must have been well aware that he could make no progress to the northward in Baffin's Bay, but his double pay of a Post-Captain of the Royal Navy, to which he had been fortuitously elevated, began earlier, and he had an object in visiting Uppernavik, to procure from this northernmost of the Danish settlements, the services of his friend, Mr. Petersen, whom he induced to leave his situation of £20 a year (with which he was dissatisfied), for the position of interpreter with him at £75 a year, and without the Danish Governor's permission. In the month of August, the *Felix* overtook the whole of the Government ships, when about the 12th of that month the aboriginal Esquimaux were seen on the margin of the land-ice, and had on the preceding day been communicated with by Captain Penny, and whose note delivered by them to the officers of the *Intrepid* and *Felix*, for Captain Austin, proved that no inquiries had been made respecting the fate of the missing ships. Adam Beck, the interpreter of the *Felix*, having obtained information from the stranger Esquimaux, which he could not fully communicate (the *Felix* being then at a distance), Captain Penny's interpreter was sent for, and flatly contradicted the statement of Adam Beck, calling him " a liar," which being ironically repeated by the poor fellow, who was frightened (and no wonder, as it is well known that these Danish overseers are often severe on the poor natives of Greenland). In the meantime a young Esquimaux was brought on board the *Assistance*, and being tutored by Petersen, also denied the truth of Adam Beck's story, and every one, as well as myself, believed it was a fabrication, although no one could conjecture why he should, in a moment, have conjured up such a story ; and Petersen's motive did not, at that time, become apparent. We all proceeded on our voyage, arrangements having been made that Captain Penny, according to his instructions, was to visit and examine Jones's Sound (which indeed was the origin of his being employed), and the others to examine the positions within Barrow's Strait; but Captain Penny did not wait near Jones's Sound for its opening, which could not be expected for some days, but proceeded up Lancaster Sound, where he spoke the *North Star*, and by her his despatches were sent home, among others, a letter from Mr. Petersen to his wife at Uppernavik, which will be noticed hereafter. We subsequently communicated with each other at Union Bay, Beechey Island, where Captain Penny, unjustly to Captain Phillips and Mr. Abernethy, appropriated to himself the credit of discovering the graves of the deceased men that had belonged to the *Erebus* and *Terror*. Having remained in the Wellington Channel two days longer than any other vessel, the *Felix*, owing to a disruption of a part of the edge of the barrier which crossed, we were enabled distinctly to see land to the north of this barrier, which I named " North Victoria," but which was subsequently claimed by Captain Penny as his discovery, and named "Albert Land." After passing Wellington Channel, and ascertaining that the passage between Griffith's and Cornwallis Islands was closed by ice for the season, we were returning to Wellington Channel with the intention of obtaining a position as far north as I could, when we unfortunately fell in with Captain Penny, who informed us that Captain Austin's squadron were proceeding to a bay discovered in Cornwallis Island, to which we accompanied the *Lady Franklin* and *Sophia*, expecting that, as nothing more could be done that season, I should be requested to return to England with despatches. On the following day we were finally frozen in, and Captain Austin's squadron did not reach our harbour.

During the whole winter, Adam Beck continued to assert the truth of his statement respecting the fate of Sir John Franklin, and as he began to understand English, explanations and information were elicited from him that convinced almost all on board the *Felix* that he had told the truth. Before leaving our position at Cornwallis Island, I had several conversations in the Danish language, which he understands, which convinced me that there was at least so much probability in his report, as demanded that a search in that locality should be made for the wreck of the missing ships.

It was therefore my determination to endeavour, even with the slender means and small quantity of provisions I possessed, to make the search, which seemed to give much delight to Adam Beck, who exclaimed, "Now you see I not tell a lie !" I communicated to Captain Penny that I intended going round the north side of the main ice, and land Adam Beck at Disco, where I hoped to find the provisions directed to be landed there by the *North Star*, and he communicated to me (in presence of several persons) that he believed the missing ships had been wrecked on the west coast of Baffin's Bay ; and, as he had an interpreter, he would examine the whole coast between Lancaster Sound and Cumberland Strait, a distance of 600 miles, and knowing, in that case, he could not reach England before November, I sent no despatches by him. We proceeded to carry our intentions into execution, but found that the land ice, from the latitude of 77° to 74°, extended thirty miles from the east coast, and as we were unprepared to winter, having only three months' provisions left, we had no alternative but to proceed to Godhavn, in Disco Island, where we hoped to obtain a supply that would enable us to return to the northward. On approaching Disco (which we found quite clear of ice) we fell in with the Danish Government store-ship *Hyalfisken*, Captain Humble, who kindly piloted us into Godhavn. On our arrival I discharged Adam Beck, and in conversation with Captain Humble, I obtained the following astounding information. Captain Humble said :—"I have just come from Uppernavik, and have seen Mr. Petersen's wife, who had received a letter from her husband, dated July, Lancaster Sound (which I read), saying that it was now certain that they would comfortably spend the winter in some snug harbour, and as he would be carried to England and spend another winter there, he would have plenty of money from the English Government, and that he would come out with Captain Penny, who would have the command of another expedition, and come home to Copenhagen, desiring her to sell her furniture, &c. Another came to the wife's sister, who is married to the mate of one of the Government ships —hoping that Petersen would be carried to England, as in that case, he would return with sufficient money to enable him to quit this wretched country." Thus it appears that Captain Penny's plans, which it is evident he attempted to put into execution, by making the best of his way home, had been organized as early as the 23rd July 1850, but as he could not have left England with the addition of a steamer before the 1st October 1851, it was impossible he could have reached the Wellington Channel that season. His object must have been, therefore, to have comfortably wintered at Ball's River, or Holsteinsborg, or some port in Greenland, on full pay (£800 a year), and proceed in June 1852, and would have been just as far forward as though he had left England at that time. His plans were, however, happily frustrated by the absence of the First Lord of the Admiralty, and the decision of the Arctic Committee.

In the meantime, Adam Beck voluntarily appeared before the resident at Godhavn, and deposed as to the truth of his former statement, subsequent to which he was examined by Inspector-general Lewis Platon, who has written to me that he is fully convinced that Adam Beck has spoken the truth.

The following is an extract of the third letter on the subject which I have received from Mr. Platon :—

"Montebello, Feb. 17, 1852.

"From the interest I take in the question where Sir John Franklin ought to be sought, and being, as you know, most decidedly of opinion that Sir John Franklin was lost on his intended return, I feel myself bound to say a few words on this subject, which you will use as you think proper.

" I shall merely premise what you are already aware of, that I have, during four years and a half, held a responsible government situation in Greenland. Three years of this time I resided at Holsteinsborg, and had thus ample opportunity of observing the character of the natives generally, and of Adam Beck individually, as he during that time never omitted an opportunity of thrusting himself into my notice, and he several times, temporarily, was attached to my household. I think therefore I may, without presumption, claim to be considered as not incompetent to judge of what confidence there ought to be placed in what may be deduced from such a document as his. From my knowledge of the character of Adam Beck, I may safely assert, that it is beyond doubt that he has heard something about the two lost ships; but certainly it would be difficult to say what it is he has heard, merely by reading his deposition. As I informed you in a former letter, I have seen this man after his discharge at Godhavn; I therefore look on the deposition in a far different manner than others unacquainted with these facts undoubtedly would do; and I maintain that it throws a light on the fate of Sir John and his gallant crew, and that it would be shameful altogether to reject his evidence. I cannot but regret that you did not get a copy of the other deposition he made, as it was far more satisfactory than the one you got. I must make haste to be in time for post that leaves here at two o'clock, and must therefore conclude, angry with myself for not being able to write such as to convince any but myself that the greater reliance may be placed on his assertion. Pray write me as soon as possible, and believe me, &c., &c.

(Signed)   " L. PLATON."

Mr. Platon's former letters, with my own, have been sent to the late Admiralty. In one of them he says, " The people of Denmark think it strange that the English Government are sending to search for Franklin in every place but where he is to be found."

Captain Penny must no longer assert that I am the only person who gives any credit to Adam Beck's assertion; but in return I must be permitted to say, that I yield not the smallest credit to the assertion of Captain Penny, that Sir John Franklin ever went up the Wellington Channel. I was present at the interview he had with Captain Austin on board the *Resolute*, on the 11th of August, when I can testify that Captain Penny made no application at that time for a steam-vessel; moreover, I can testify that the application for a steam-vessel would have been absurd, as it was quite impossible she could have proceeded up that channel. The *Felix* was the last vessel that left that spot on the 13th of August, at which time the barrier of ice was still across it; on

that day, no water could be seen from Cape Spencer to the northward, and then Captain Penny's vessels were both to the eastward of Cape Riley. Captain Penny asserts that Captain Austin
took the *Felix* in tow to take her home, that she might take the
credit of his discoveries; but the truth is, that Captain Austin
offered to tow Captain Penny's vessels out of Lancaster Sound,
which offer he did not accept; and it was then that he offered to
take us as far as Union Bay, Beechey Island, where Captain Penny
must have seen the *Felix* as he passed.

I have now only one more subject to disabuse. Captain Penny's
whole idea that Sir John Franklin went up the Wellington
Channel, was based on the fact of his having found upon the ice
two chips of wood, which I verily believe must have been thrown
on the ice by some of his own crew, for otherwise they would have
been found sunk considerably below the surface, and they were
such pieces of wood as were numerous where the ships wintered.
But if Captain Penny really believed that the missing ships had
gone up what he now calls the Victoria Channel (not marked as
such in the chart he gave to me), why did he not remain himself
to explore it in the spring?—He ventured to say that he had not
enough of provisions, because he had given some to the *Felix;*
but this he denied on the Committee, as two cwt. of carrots and
a bag of potatoes were all we got, and for which we would have
supplied him with ten tons of coals, and six casks of flour; but
Captain Austin would certainly have supplied him up to three
years; besides the depôt at Leopold Island was within sixty miles
of where his vessel would be. When I said in my evidence that
Captains Austin and Penny were both justified in coming home,
it was with the conviction that they both thought and believed
that the locality was completely searched, and that they both
believed (as I do) that the missing ships never went up that
Channel. I have no doubt that they lost both seasons of 1845
and 1846, and that finding they had only provisions for another
year (and perhaps less, as many of Goldner's canisters were found
with only one cut at the top, which being convex were clear
proofs of their putrescent condition), that they were lost on the
passage home. Captain Penny's assertion (page 10), that the loss
of two ships with the whole crews is next to impossible, and contrary to all experience; this observation cannot apply to ships
wrecked in Baffin's Bay; after the month of September there is
no experience of any ships being lost in Baffin's Bay, but in the
summer.

In conclusion, I deeply regret that Captain Penny has been so
imprudent as to publish what he has done; I believed that he
really had been actuated by feelings of philanthropy, touching
the rescue of my gallant friend Franklin and his brave com-

panions ; he had at one time gained my esteem and regard, and he knows that I acted as a peacemaker between him and those whom his virulent temper had offended. I was an admirer of his zeal and unflinching perseverance, and I then believed that he had no sinister motive ; it has been, therefore, with mixed feelings of sorrow and of pity that I have been constrained to change my opinion of an individual who has proved that he ought not to have been elevated to the position in which he was unfortunately placed.

(Signed) JOHN ROSS, Rear-Admiral.

No. 7.

Admiralty, 13th March, 1852.

SIR,

I have received and laid before my Lords Commissioners of the Admiralty your letter of the 10th instant, with its enclosure, on the subject of Adam Beck's deposition relative to the missing ships under the orders of Captain Sir John Franklin.

I am, &c.

(Signed) AUGUSTUS STAFFORD.

Rear Admiral Sir John Ross, C.B.

No. 8.

267, Strand, London, 23rd March, 1852..

SIR,

Enclosed you will receive the extract of a letter I have this day received from Inspector-general Lewis Platon, touching the fate of Sir John Franklin's expedition, which I am to request that you will be pleased to lay before the Lords Commissioners of the Admiralty for their Lordships' serious consideration, and to inform their Lordships that I entirely agree with the Danish Inspector-general that there is no chance of deciding the question of the missing ships but by the examination I have recommended.

I have, &c.

(Signed) JOHN ROSS, Rear-Admiral.

To Captain W. A. B. Hamilton, R.N., &c. &c. &c.

Enclosure to No. 8.

Extract of a Letter from the Danish Inspector-General of Greenland touching the Fate of Sir John Franklin's Expedition.

Montebello, Denmark, 5th March, 1852.

MY DEAR SIR,

Yours of the 26th ult. I had the pleasure of receiving this day. I am really both surprised and vexed that nothing yet has been decided on. The season is already far advanced, and it is time Government should decide whether they will indeed search after Sir John Franklin in earnest, or if they intend to rest satisfied with sending the expedition under Sir Edward Belcher in a direction where others have failed in tracing the unfortunate voyagers farther than Beechey Island, and where the chances are a thousand to one that the expedition will return as wise as they leave. I really do hope the Government will pay less attention to the representations of others, and listen somewhat more to the voice of reason. The people of England are strangely infatuated as regards this question.

The more I think, and the more I put this and that together, the more convinced I am that Sir John Franklin never committed such an act of madness as to push his way farther on, after leaving Beechey Island, having most likely at the time, scarcely provisions enough left for the space of time it had taken him to reach this place. Don't tell me about his procuring, and with ease too, such a lot of provisions as the officers of the different expedition ships seem to lay such weight upon. I know the country too well for that ; but even suppose they could get an inexhaustible supply of birds, had he salt enough to cure such a number? Still an Englishman is no Esquimaux, and no one but an Esquimaux or a Russian can live and do his duty on board any length of time on such a diet, in such a climate Sir John was too old a hand in those regions not to know that, and it is my firm belief that having made up his mind to return to England, he was lost on his home passage.

Should you consider my presence in England likely to forward the cause, pray let me know, as I take a very deep interest in the solution of the question. I wish to Heaven that your next would contain the joyful intelligence that Government had at last decided in your favour, as I feel confident that it will be the only expedition with any chance of success.

I remain, &c.

(Signed)   L. PLATON.

No. 9.

Admiralty, 26th March, 1852.

Sir,

I have received and laid before my Lords Commissioners of the Admiralty your letter of the 23rd instant, with its enclosures, respecting the further search after Sir John Franklin's expedition.

I am, &c.

W. A. B. HAMILTON.

Rear Admiral Sir John Ross, C.B.

(D.)

By the Commissioners for executing the Office of Lord High Admiral of the United Kingdom of Great Britain and Ireland, &c. &c.

1. Her Majesty's Government having determined that further endeavours shall be made to trace the progress of Her Majesty's ships *Erebus* and *Terror*, under the command of Sir John Franklin, and to resume the search after that expedition,—and, having resolved to employ you in the command of the two vessels, the *Lady Franklin* and *Sophia*, which have been equipped for that service—you are hereby required and directed, so soon as the said vessels shall be in all respects ready for sea, to proceed with them with all due dispatch to Davis's Strait.

2. In entrusting you with the above command, we do not deem it advisable to furnish you with minute instructions as to the course you are to pursue.—In accepting your offer of service, regard has been had to your long experience in Arctic Navigation, and to the attention you had evidently paid to the subject of the missing ships. We deem it expedient rather, that you should be instructed in all the circumstances of the case, and that you should be left to the exercise of your own judgment and discretion, in combining the most active and energetic search after Her Majesty's ships *Erebus* and *Terror*, with a strict and careful regard to the safety of the ships and their crews under your charge: and with a fixed attention to that part of your orders which relate to your returning with those ships to this country.

3. For this purpose, you will be furnished with copies of the original instructions given to Sir John Franklin, and which instructions will indicate the course he was directed to pursue, together with our orders and directions to Sir James Ross, when

I

he was despatched on a search after Sir John Franklin, in the spring of 1848.

4. You will be aware that the case virtually stands now as it did then.—Sir James Ross, from adverse circumstances, failed in discovering traces of the missing Expedition.

5. Our orders of the 9th May, 1848, to Sir James Ross, will still serve as the indication of our views of the general course you will have to pursue ; but, it being our desire that a certain Strait, known as Alderman Jones's Sound, and which would not appear to have been as yet examined, should be searched ; you are hereby required and directed to proceed in the first instance to that Sound, closely examining the shores for any traces of Sir John Franklin's course, and proceeding, should it offer the means of your doing so, in the direction of *Wellington Strait*, and *on to the Parry Islands and Melville Island.*

6. On your proceeding in the above direction, too much vigilance cannot be observed in your search along the various shores, for traces of the missing Expedition ; at the same time you will bear in mind that Sir John Franklin's orders were " to push on through Lancaster Sound, without stopping to examine any openings north or south of that Sound, till he had reached Cape Walker." And although it may be possible that the obstructions, incident to navigation in those seas, may have forced Sir John Franklin north or south of his prescribed course, yet that his principal object would be, the gaining the latitude and longitude of Cape Walker.

7. To that point, therefore, failing your discovering traces of the Expedition in your course by Jones's Sound and the Parry Islands, your efforts will be directed, and beyond this, your own judgment must be your principal guide.

8. The circumstance of Sir James Ross having partially searched the shores of Lancaster Sound and Barrow's Strait, as far west as Cape Rennell, without discovering traces of Sir John Franklin's ships, has led, in some quarters, to the supposition of an extreme case, viz. :—that, failing to get into Lancaster Sound, Sir John Franklin had proceeded in the direction of Smith's Sound, at the head of Baffin's Bay.

9. We do not deem it expedient to direct your attention specially to this Sound (or supposed Sound) ; but should your passage by Jones's Sound, to which you *are* specially directed, be early and absolutely impeded, and there should appear to you to be the time (without hazarding the only remaining chance of proceeding to Wellington Strait, the Parry Islands, and Cape Walker by Lancaster Sound,) for examining Smith's Sound, you are at liberty to do so ; but this is a contingency scarcely to be contemplated : as, in the event of your being frustrated in the attempt to get to the westward, and towards Wellington Strait by Jones's

Sound,—the late period of the year when Smith's Sound is said to be open, would render it difficult, if not impossible, to combine a search in that quarter, with the securing a passage into Lancaster Sound before the season closed.

10. Much of the painful anxiety that now exists respecting the missing Ships might possibly have been avoided, if greater care had been taken to leave traces of their progress. You will consider it rigidly your duty, and a matter of the utmost importance, that every means should be adopted for marking your own track.

For this purpose you will provide yourself with an ample supply of red and white lead for making paint; and in addition to the usual pole or staff, or cairn of stones, usually looked for on a cape or headland, you will, wherever the colouring of the cliff or shore admits of a mark being made in strong relief, paint a red or white cross, as the case may be, depositing as near to its base as possible, and at right angles with the perpendicular part of such cross, a bottle or other vessel containing a short summary of your proceedings up to the date of the deposit; an account of the state of your supplies and resources, the health of your party, and your further intended course.

11. There remains but to caution you as to your return with your ships to this country.

These ships have been provisioned and stored for three years; but you will bear in mind that this liberal supply is to meet contingencies separate, on the one hand, from the victualling of your own people, and, on the other, from a needless, reckless, and hazardous continuance in the Arctic regions.

You have been victualled to supply the missing Expedition, or any part of it you may providentially discover—here is the one contingency; unforeseen impediments, or a certain prospect of coming up with any part of the missing Expedition compelling you to pass a second winter in the ice, is another; but our directions to you are—1st, to use your utmost endeavours (consistent with the safety of the lives of those entrusted to your command,) to succour in *this summer* the party under Sir John Franklin, taking care to secure your winter quarters in good time; and, 2nd, that the same active endeavours will be used by you in the ensuing summer of 1851, to secure the return of your own ships to this country.

12. We refer you to the instructions contained in par. 21 of Sir John Franklin's orders, for your guidance in the event of one of your ships being disabled; or in case of any accident to yourself; and in par. 22 of the same orders, are full instructions as to transmitting reports of your progress to our Secretary, for our information, to both of which you will strictly attend.

13. In conclusion, we have only to repeat the expressions of

our confidence in your skill, and in your known ardour in a generous cause; and we commend you, and those with you, to a good Providence, with our earnest wishes for your success.

Given under our hands this 11th April, 1850,

(Signed)   F. T. BARING.
J. H. D. DUNDAS.

By Command of their Lordships,
W. A. B. HAMILTON.

Mr. William Penny, ship "Lady Franklin,"
in charge of an Expedition to the Arctic Seas, at Aberdeen.

Admiralty, April 10, 1850.

SIR,

I am commanded by my Lords Commissioners of the Admiralty to send you herewith the original and duplicate of a letter addressed to Mr. Saunders, Master, commanding Her Majesty's Store Ship *North Star*, in the Arctic Seas, containing instructions for his guidance, one of which my Lords request you will take charge of yourself, for delivery to that officer, should you fall in with him; and the other you are to put in the possession of Mr. Stewart, of the ship *Sophia*, for the same purpose.

I have, &c.

(Signed)   W. A. B. HAMILTON.

Captain Penny, ship "Lady Franklin," Aberdeen.

Admiralty, April 10, 1850.

SIR,

I am commanded by my Lords Commissioners of the Admiralty to acquaint you,

1. That Sir James Ross having returned to England in the month of November last, without having discovered any traces of the Missing Expedition under Sir John Franklin's orders, and the necessity for the stores and provisions with which he was charged being deposited as directed being all the more urgent, my Lords can only trust that you have been able to land them accordingly.

2. That as our last Reports from you were dated 19th July, 1849, lat. 74° 3′, long. 59° 40′, W., the anxiety on the part of

their Lordships to receive further intelligence of your proceedings is great; and they can therefore only hope, in the event of this despatch reaching you, and of your not having succeeded in affording succour to any of Sir John Franklin's party, that it may find you returning with Her Majesty's ship under your command to England.

3. And that in order that you may be in full possession of all that has occurred, or that has been done since your departure, relative to the relief of Sir John Franklin, you are herewith furnished with a printed return which will put you in complete possession of the state of the case; and to which my Lords have only to add, that four ships under the command of Captain Austin, two of them being auxiliary steam-vessels, are now fitting at Woolwich; in addition to the two vessels under Captain Penny's orders, and by which this despatch is sent, for the purpose of continuing the search after Sir John Franklin's Expedition (irrespective of private expeditions from this country and the United States); and that as supplies of stores, especially coals, would be most needful for these vessels, as an auxiliary, you are to land at the Whale Fish Islands, or at Disco, whatever proportion of coals or provisions you consider you can with propriety spare, returning without loss of time to England.

I am, &c.

(Signed)   W. A. B. HAMILTON.

Mr. James Saunders,
Master Commanding H.M.S. "North Star."

THE END.

Letter referred to in pp. 18 *and* 49.

27th November, 1849.

I shall not trouble my Lords Commissioners of the Admiralty with a detailed refutation of the published opinions given by the several officers in favour of large ships being employed in the Arctic regions instead of small vessels, as the question must now have been sufficiently decided by the recent failure of the *Enterprize* and *Investigator*, proposed by them in the place of the four small vessels recommended, which would have not only extended the search and carried an equal quantity of provisions, but would have been more efficiently navigated with half the number of men and at half the expense, while it would have saved the necessity of despatching the now missing ship with supplies, and at half the expense. And it is to be regretted that their Lordships were led, by those who were by them supposed to know what was best, into that unfortunate determination.

But I must beg leave to state, and that too from experience, that Captain Beechy's objections to the use of a steam vessel among ice are totally without foundation, and could only have arisen from his consummate ignorance of the subject. My little steam vessel, the *Victory*, was fitted with paddle-wheels (which Captain Beechy never saw) of a peculiar construction, for use among ice; they could be taken entirely out of danger by two men in less than a minute, and the sponsons, instead of endangering the vessel, contributed mainly to her safety, the ice coming under them in a collision (which was often the case in the *Victory*), assisted the vessel in rising up to the pressure, instead of being crushed by it, on which mainly depends her safety. And the engine itself, being fixed totally independent of the straining of the vessel, can receive no injury whatever from the distortion of her frame. The only further observation I think it necessary to make, is, that (page 46) Sir James Ross's assertion in contradiction to Dr. King, that " Barrow Strait was not ice-bound in 1832," is a wilful misrepresentation of the fact, and can be contradicted by Sergeant Park, of the E division of Police, Robert Shreeve, of Lower Seymour-street, and Thomas Abernethy; and it is also true, that on that year and several others, no ship could get up Barrow Strait for ice, where at length he himself found it unnavigable. Provisions being already stored at Whaler Point, the following vessels only will be required, the expense of which, the sale of the *Enterprize* and *Investigator*, which are only fit for employment in the whale fishery, would more than cover.

JOHN ROSS.